Dream
House

Also by Charlotte Nekola

Writing Red: An Anthology of American Women Writers, 1930–1940
(coedited with Paula Rabinowitz)

Dream House

A Memoir

Charlotte
Nekola

W·W·Norton & Company

New York   London

The text of this book is composed in 12/14.5 Centaur
with the display set in Centaur
Composition and Manufacturing by the Maple-Vail Book Manufacturing Group.
Book design by Margaret Wagner

Library of Congress Cataloging-in-Publication Data
Nekola, Charlotte.
Dream house : a memoir / Charlotte Nekola. — 1st ed.
p.   cm.
1. Nekola, Charlotte.   2. Middle West — Biography.   3. Saint Louis
(Mo.) — Biography.   I. Title.
CT275.N416A3   1992
977'.03'092 — dc20   92-9617

ISBN 0-393-03433-X

W. W. Norton & Company, Inc., 500 Fifth Avenue, New York, N.Y. 10110
W. W. Norton & Company Ltd., 10 Coptic Street, London WC1A 1PU
1   2   3   4   5   6   7   8   9   0

For Anna and Aaron

Contents

Grateful Acknowledgment to:

The one who let me run in the ravine, the one who named plants for me, the one who sang at night, the one who taught me the broad jump, the one who laid out the green bowls for breakfast, the ones who wait for me across a table, the ones who wait for me now at home.

Elmaz Abinader, Wesley Blixt, Barbara Bracey, Rob Cohen, Abigail Connell, Joanna Ekman, Alice Echols, Bob Franchi, Cara Franchi, Sarah Hawrylak, Dan Hoffman, Betsey Lerner, Joanna Mauer, Patti McAskin, Ashton Nichols, Kimberley Nichols, Barney Pace, Paula Rabinowitz, Connie Samaras, Meryl Schneider, Susan West, for readings and friendship.

Amy Cherry, a most thoughtful editor.
Robert Ready, for twenty years of encouragement.
Toni Morrison, for extending the Schweitzer Fellowship in Humanities to me, and for a conversation about "permission to write."
Florence Howe, Jason Epstein, Stanley Plumly, Walter and Joan Politzer, for encouragement.
Baer's Patisserie, Englewood, New Jersey, especially Nettie and Florence, and George and Alex at La Bonne Patisserie, Tenafly, New Jersey, for a place to write.

Doris Howard, Barbara Suter, and the Al-Anon-ACOA groups.

Delia Webster and Aspex, for technical assistance.

Kathie Mazure, for help with my children.

Department of English, William Paterson College, for its support;
William Paterson College, for release time.

John Nekola, for many kinds of help.

Anna Nekola Politzer, Aaron Nekola Politzer, the Rundle family,
Gina Urani, and Tom Urani, for their presence.

Roger Politzer, for something unusual.

You cannot fold a Flood —
And put it in a Drawer —
Because the Winds would find it out —
And tell your Cedar Floor.

— EMILY DICKINSON

Dream
House

Family Stories

THE story went that my great-grandfather settled east of St. Louis in the 1860s on top of an Indian mound. He built a farmhouse there, in what is now called the Cahokia Mounds State Historic Site. The mound rises out of flat river-basin land. From the top, you can see the profiles of rivers and cities for 360 degrees. It was said that the Moenck side of the family, my father's mother's side, the ones who kept her in horses but no shoes, built their farmhouse right on top of this land. It became known as Monk's Mound. So the story went. My grandmother and her sister Minnie posed in front of the mound for a group portrait in 1926. In print dresses to their ankles, heavy black shoes like nurses wore, hats with droopy flowers, they stand in front with their arms laced together. They look expectant and pleased with themselves, the way people do on an outing. Maybe even a little smug, as when people too poor to wear shoes own something of their own, even if they took it away from someone else. Their very own mound, they thought.

The oddness, and the politics of a German immigrant family claiming a Native American solar observatory as their own, the Stonehenge of the Missouri-Illinois river basin, had certainly entered no one's mind. My father confidently wrote in a biographical essay for night school at age twenty-one that there was "a stately farmhouse just below the bluffs, on the road from Collinsville, Illinois. That house, built upon a truncated Indian mound by William the

Elder, served as a home for Friederich Moenck and his wife and their daughters." My grandmother was one of the daughters, and so was Aunt Minnie. So there it was — the family story, the family mound.

I was only dimly aware of this story growing up. My Great-Aunt Minnie, who was very old, still lived in Edwardsville, Illinois, in the 1950s. We paid a visit once and found a faded frame house, overgrown bridal-wreath bushes, picket fences, ticking clocks, dark linoleum, and lace throws on the backs of skeleton chairs. My father mentioned the mounds on the way there and stopped the car. I was a five-year-old dressed for visiting, a plaid dress with a white collar, patent-leather Mary Jane shoes, stepping out of a pink car with fins, in the warm sunlight of March, on the still-cold ground. Stepping out and squinting at what looked like a big hill with a flat top, something like a flattop haircut. It made only a passing impression, a little interesting, a little boring, like most things your parents stopped the car to point out.

Many years later, after my father died, my brother got the idea that the mounds might have something to offer us. He started to visit them and did some research in the county land deeds office. It seemed that the family story of the mounds was pure fabrication. The only recorded Moencks who lived near this mound were Trappist monks, who went there to convert the Indians. No Moencks were listed in the land deeds office. Perhaps they owned no land, but had horses. Or no horses, or shoes either. It had been a nice story, useful in linking the shoeless, wandering Nekolas to something older, something of history, something of permanence, even if it wasn't ours. There were hundreds of mounds, but Monk's Mound, the one Matilda and Minnie posed next to in the snapshot, hadn't been part of the family in any official way.

My brother visited the mounds often, anyway. He said it was a spiritual place for him. He took to going there every other Sunday or so. It was only twenty minutes from his little house in Dogtown. The trip involved a bridge across the Mississippi and a river road, which made him happy. When I visited him there in St. Louis four years after my father died, he wanted to take me there. I was not in the mood to be stirred, spiritually or otherwise. It was enough to be back in St. Louis, my old city of bricks, again. But I was curious. It was a Sunday night in November, with dark sheets of rain outside. We crossed the flat face of the bridge, a muddy swath of river panning out beneath it, long barges stationed beneath. The road to the mounds is old Route 40. It still offers motels that look like tiny log cabins or white bungalows, some half-lit neon signs for food or lumberyards. The mounds stood up over the dark fields. The rain threatened to flood, and we had one three-dollar umbrella from Taiwan between us. I resisted those mounds, as I do any matter of spirit, an old habit.

But once we were up there, my breath caught. From the top of the mound, you see a lot of highways, but also the ravines of cottonwood and persimmon, the tumbling approach down a bluff to a river basin, the fields full of the same sumac and milkweed that followed my childhood days. The tender slice of water, hard to come by in so much muddy flatland, so many roots of sassafras. Looking longer, you could see all the cities, large and small, that dotted the conversation of my parents, half heard and half ignored, the names of cities too boring to be remembered but unforgettable all the same. Homely names, full of children playing in the dust — Edwardsville, Collinsville. Children about to fall in quarries — Granite City. Or the sweetheart of everyone's youth, the place where everyone went for real work and real life, and beer gardens, meat, smoke, trolleys, train yards, and shoes — St. Louis.

Suddenly, on top of the mound of family history, the not-heirloom heirloom mound, I could see the history, the migrations, the sphere of operation. My father, the skinny pencil-wielding tyrant of my household, was only a small-town boy, first from Edwards-ville, then Collinsville, so enthralled with Collinsville Elementary School that he held on to a picture postcard of it, in all its inde-structible brick-upon-brick glory, until he died. The same town where he wrote that Ma and Pa sat on the porch in the evening when the work was done. A creaky wood porch, I am sure, the mud swept off every day with a bit of venom and the outdoor broom. He said there was a bed of four-o'clocks there, and toads.

It seemed like such a harmless story, how could so much harm have resulted? You tell the story like this: A skinny boy from Col-linsville, his mother the daughter of a farming rapscallion who bought her horses, but no shoes. His father a stout carpenter who liked a good time, and didn't see much point in working too hard. It was his mother who stood the slight boy by a blackboard at age four, in Collinsville, and taught him the alphabet, some river driving in her. Once she had had another child, a girl named Evelyn with long wavy hair, before she was married to my grandfather. Her husband had gone crazy and come to kill her. But she was out working, washing another woman's floor. He found Evelyn instead.

Now my grandmother is the river force who convinces her new husband to move to St. Louis in 1914, when everything was being built out of brick, houses and factories down street after street. They built half a house for themselves using the wall of a relative's house for one of their own. The father has many houses to build. He even works on the elephant house at Forest Park Zoo, and by the 1920s, they own two cars. The slight son runs down the street at lunchtime with sandwiches wrapped in paper, cervelat sausage with strawberry preserves, to be eaten by father and son in the plain silence of the noontime sun, sitting on a curb or a pile of bricks.

In 1926, my grandfather died suddenly, a hard death from lung cancer in St. Louis. The sky, as usual, was full of smoke. On his deathbed, he tells my father not to be a carpenter, that he's too slight for heavy work, and to learn mechanical drawing instead. My father takes his advice. He sharpens other people's pencils, learns mechanical drawing, drops out of school for ten years right through the Depression. He and his mother weather those years together, renting out flats in their home on Penrose Street. "We couldn't keep them if they couldn't pay eighteen dollars a month, because then we couldn't keep ourselves," he said. He takes himself to night school, church youth group, church drama group, gets an offer to go away to seminary, but his mother talks him out of it. Who would take care of her? He stays home and fixes up the electrical outlets and windowsills, eats meat sometimes at Penrose Street. The years get better; he falls in love with the WPA, the TVA, and a nun. Then he meets my mother, with the improbable name of Beryl, who, he says happily, "swam like a seal."

THE story of my mother's side of the family can be told like this: My great-grandfather was a saloonkeeper in St. Louis, who lived with his family upstairs. My grandfather was the earnest type, and somehow worked his way into dental school at Washington University. He met my grandmother, the beautiful but lame Estella, on a streetcar and courted her patiently for six years until he graduated. Then he rented an office on Grand Avenue and became a man with a large house. They had two daughters, whom they named Beryl and Lois. The Depression moved them down to Hebert Street, which was still very respectable. Despite his losses in the stock market and the patients he treated for free, or for baskets of eggs or tomatoes, his family did not suffer. They sent their daughters to college. My grandmother even had a "girl" from Arkansas, named Crystal, to help with the house, the kind of work my father's mother had been doing back in Illinois, on the day her daughter got shot instead of her.

So my father moved up to my mother and her solid-looking family on Hebert Street. The front door of the house was made of heavy oak with thick leaded glass. After they married, my parents' ideals involved traveling away from my grandmothers, one known to be "severe," the other known to be "bitter." Traveling away from the dusty porch in Collinsville, traveling away from a backyard in Edwardsville, traveling away from the soot of downtown St. Louis. Traveling away from the boy just off from work, in night school, a boy smoking cigarettes and hopping freight cars in the trainyards on Saturday afternoon to spite his mother, whom he supported with his labor. From the girl who hesitated, before she put her hand against the windowpane. They would travel away, and send their children ahead. It wasn't a new story, it was the same story, of families restless for the next thing, hungry for the future moment, maybe not paying attention to the present moment. Maybe not in their life as it surrounded them, or in the sun of noontime, the rain of an afternoon.

My father wanted to forget not just what happened, but how he felt walking into a room full of people or showing his work. But mostly he wanted to forget the thin voice of his mother, always disappointed. Or the voice of his father, saying that he couldn't lay bricks, or maybe the story of the lost sister with the wavy hair. My mother was glad not to hear her mother, at the bottom of the kitchen stairs, telling her to come down again, and sew her French knots right this time.

So people always move, and try to put the past behind them, and set forth a new and better life for their children. Now, my mother, in good clothes, picked up my father's shirts at the laundry, in a car with fins. A small girl rode in the backseat. The two older children were in class in their good public school and would someday go to college. The shirts were pinned to pieces of cardboard and stacked up well in his suitcase next to the fifth of Old Crow.

The stories he brought home were always about traveling, not about where he was sitting, at his table. There were many ways in America to call this success.

FROM the top of the mound, my brother and I could see the whole S-shaped sweep of our family's migration: Edwardsville, Collinsville, St. Louis, Normandy. All anyone had ever tried to do, it seemed, was to move on, to find something better for the children. From the top of the mound, the path of the family's journey seemed clear, an innocent trip. From Czechoslovakia, from Germany, to the river-bluff towns of Illinois, to St. Louis for the real money, city life, education. A city kind of job for the son, the one who stood next to a chalkboard with his mother at age four. The son moved from Penrose Street to the north part of the suburbs, to a brick house with a field behind it. He and his children and their dog could forage for newly frostbitten persimmons and for thorny blackberries, see possums hanging in trees, or even grow a patch of tall corn out back. Their mother could watch them run to the field from the kitchen window; she could stand at the front door as they walked down the sidewalk to school. On weekends, the family would drive to the city for the Art Museum, or the Ethical Culture Society, or Grandmother's house for Sunday dinner. They would not go back to the city to buy moldy country hams at the Soulard Market, or catfish from Arkansas, or new corn from the flatlands, or to work a machine at Anheuser-Busch, or to glue shoes together at Bata.

In the suburbs, the children would be readied for college, that other realm of gold. The children would be sent ahead to a place where the father could never go, a life with no memory of fixing other people's faucets on Penrose Street, working in laundries, being ashamed because you were skinny and couldn't hold up beams, listening to a widow's worries over a plate of ham hocks. They would set their children out, the way people set out plants, to see if they could root. Like the story of the mound, it was a story that no one knew enough about.

Red

MY grandmother on my mother's side was kindly toward us, but stiff. It came as one of the greatest surprises of my lifetime to learn that she had once been nicknamed Red. I was stunned to think that she could have had red hair. She was seventy when I was born, and always appeared with a snowy cap of slightly blue-rinsed hair. Was it possible, then, that she had ever looked different, pinned up red tresses on top of her head? The almost complete absence of toys in her house, the way she held her happiness in at seeing us, shyly, as if embarrassed, and her bossiness with my mother over hemlines, or how to cook a pot roast, made her earlier incarnation as the lighthearted and flamboyant Red most improbable.

She was noted for not understanding jokes and did not take teasing well. Once she visited our house and brought the usual two loaves of homemade bread. But that week her baking was off, and the bread fell apart as it was sliced. My brother's twelve-year-old friend Warren was over at our house and sat down to taste the new loaf with my brother. "Sure is crumby," he said cheerfully, meaning the little pile of crumbs that had accumulated. Grandma didn't see the unintended irony — she was simply mortified that a boy had caught her out at less than perfect bread. It took her most of the afternoon to recover. How, then, was it possible that anyone had ever gotten away with calling her Red? It was my grandfather who thought it up, and apparently he even did things like call up the stairs, "Hey Red!" Further, from the way she told it, it was clear that she liked it. Certainly there was no explanation for the mysteries of love, especially hard to imagine in a house frozen in cut glass, African violets, couches with claw feet, ticking clocks, shades pulled down for the heat at a certain time in the morning.

Red was born in 1872 in St. Louis. This child, named Estella, must have seemed stellar: her mother was forty-seven when she gave birth to her. Estella's father was her mother's third husband. She brought six children to the marriage, and her husband also brought six children. So my grandmother was the only child of their union, born with twelve brothers and sisters ready-made. I cannot tell you how these thirteen children were fed and clothed. My grandmother once mentioned something about peeling potatoes for fourteen. About leaving school in the eighth grade because her knee was lame, and not wanting to be a burden to her mother, and becoming an apprentice to a French seamstress. Later she sewed in a factory where they made shirtwaist dresses.

These are only the barest outlines of history, which my grandmother told me one night during a thunderstorm. The outline does not tell us how everyone ate, or what they dreamed of, through the rough chapters in the story. Her mother, she said, left Germany at age sixteen. She came from a family of nine, and no one had enough to eat. So they were relieved that she would marry a man twenty years older than she, and start again in America. But sad as well — her mother took her out on the eve of her trip to look at the night sky. "We'll see the same stars," she told the daughter who'd be gone forever. The trip on the boat took six weeks, and they ate black bread and water. The newlyweds had intended to go to California on Conestoga wagons. But by the time they reached St. Louis, they decided they'd gone far enough.

The rest of the story flips by quickly, told by my grandmother according to the fate of each of my great-grandmother's husbands.

The first, the older man, took sick and died. The young widow married another, who was shot and killed in a saloon fight. The third husband was told he was going blind, and jumped out a window to his death. By this time, my great-grandmother had accumulated six children. The fourth husband was my grandmother's father. None of these men had more material wealth than a plain house and some wages, and possibly even less than that. According to the story, the source of hope during these incredible times was some kind of miracle. My grandmother's mother was illiterate, except for being able to read the texts of the Swedish mystic Emanuel Swedenborg. It was knotty material, but somehow clear to the sixteen-year-old girl who would bear seven children with four husbands.

My grandmother became a Swedenborgian as well, which was something none of us grandchildren understood very well. It was always presented to us as something to be affectionately tolerated about Grandma, the way that we tolerated her sitting down to darn socks or sew buttons on Sunday afternoons at our house, because she hated to sit still and feel useless. We knew that my grandfather found the Swedenborgians overbearing, and refused to go to church with her. So had my mother. Occasionally my grandmother took us to church with her, to a social event with iced homemade cakes, and we stood polite but aloof, humoring some old folks who wanted us to join some kind of hoax, or cult, as it seemed to us. We had been raised in Ethical Culture, a nonsectarian fellowship that taught us the seven great religions as if they were simply different kinds of folk tales, and no one any more righteous or true than the other. So Grandma's Swedenborgians always had a slightly maniacal look to us, so convinced they seemed of Their Way.

This was part of Grandma's rigidity — her dead conviction that Swedenborg was the answer. I know she was distressed that our parents didn't take us to a "real" church. It seemed to help her a great deal, but since we were raised as nonbelievers, it didn't help us a bit. At my mother's death, it just seemed to make things worse: at the gravesite, a cold and rainy day in February, when I was eleven, some church ladies came up to me, in their hats with veils, rouge on wrinkly cheeks, and fox fur collars: your mother is happy, now, they said, she's with her father. Lies, lies, I wanted to shout. How could my mother be happy if her ashes were in the ground, and I was standing there alone, thinking how ugly my shoes were?

LATER in life, when I was in my twenties, and occasionally visited Grandma overnight, we would sit up and talk for a little while after dinner. She would ask pointed, alternately tactful and invasive questions about my life. "I don't understand what you do, dear. What is this psychology you're studying? And what kind of people does Roger come from? Why don't you take a bath now?" And then maybe lapse into a few family stories about relatives I couldn't remember, offering me another piece of coconut cake, as if it were my duty to eat it. Then she'd tentatively bring out a little discussion of Swedenborg, the way you'd lure a recalcitrant alley cat in for a bite of food. She gave me his collected writings once, hoping it was something I would come to later in life, to her great relief. She told me how it gave her such comfort to know that her dead husband and daughter were still with us now.

Indeed, it must have. She lived to be ninety-three. She survived early poverty and the death of her husband. Then, a decade later, one of her daughters became inconsolable, unreachable, upon the sudden death of her husband. Within months, her other daughter, my mother, died of cancer at midlife. So she marshaled her grandchildren for family visits even after their own mothers were gone or incapable of doing so. Her daughters were lost to her. She wrote her grandchildren endless cheery and anxious letters, worried over them, knitted them hats and gloves even when they were grown-ups, sent them recipes, tracked them down, and insisted that they visit her. When we finally came, she made us pot roast dinners with cake, set a card table with a linen cloth, china, and crystal coasters for the iced-tea glasses, and got out the quilts she'd embroidered fifty years earlier.

When we weren't there, she'd find us. When I was twenty, in 1972, I dropped out of college in New Jersey to go up to New Hampshire with my boyfriend Roger and live on a farm, live the good life in a post-sixties vision of peace and harmony on the land. Our families were distressed. We weren't married. We'd dropped out of school. It didn't matter — we were following our vision, hand in hand. So we packed everything in a VW bug, camped out in a New Hampshire landfill for a week, and found a drafty two-hundred-year-old farmhouse to move into. There I was, all set to find reve-lations in the old broccoli stems I found outside in the field. I was drawing them, all day, in my new house, because I was going to go to art school and needed a portfolio, and because I didn't have the slightest idea of what else to do with myself, now that I was in New Hampshire leading the good life.

The broccoli leaves were gnarled and pocked with holes, strangely beautiful. But I felt just strange, and lost. There were ten empty rooms in this house, and Roger was out looking for work in a lumberyard, or a car bumper factory. I had spent the day before reading *The Whole Earth Catalog*. My epiphany, my transformation to the beautiful rural version, had not occurred, and what I had was an old broccoli stem and another organic peanut butter sandwich to eat. I was too mad at my parents to send them my address, but suddenly I was feeling regretful and lonesome. I had gone too far out on a limb. I forced myself from the floor, and my drawing pad, and the broccoli stalk, and went out to get the mail, my first trip to the rural delivery box at the end of my own driveway. There, a little note from Estella, who somehow had found my new address, "Dear Charlotte, How is your new house . . ." together with a recipe for pear jelly, since I was now far out in the country, and "would probably need it."

It was this kind of tenacity that I admired. She was rigid, perhaps misled, perhaps not, by her religion. She was able to do things like call the daughter ill with sadness and reclusion every Sunday, and set an egg timer for three minutes, so that she wouldn't spend too much, or perhaps be pulled too deeply into the difficulties of her daughter's emotions. But she persisted in doing this every Sunday, until she was ninety-three, and did not disappear from this daughter's landscape. She told me that in her will, she had left money specifically for my aunt to buy herself a new winter coat. My aunt always had enough money for a new coat, but Grandma was worried she'd forget or neglect herself. And so Grandma kept knitting tiny mittens for great-grandchildren even after her doctor told her her eyes were failing and she'd have to stop. She just hid the yarn and needles under her chair.

She was the one who'd saved shreds of soap, bossed Aunt Grace, Aunt Edna, and Uncle Ed, and complained to my father every week about driving "that machine" too fast. Who'd baked the same bread and cookies every week as if it were a meditation, who'd held up homemade jelly critically to the sunlight to check its clarity. Who may have made my mother too shy to teach and my aunt too fearful to answer the front door without running away. Who made me take baking soda for a stomachache, no questions about it, and had been right. Who had nothing but a hardball to play with in her house. The one who said she'd thought she'd die when her husband did, the one steeled by Swedenborg when her daughter died. The one who sensibly saved leftover fresh corn for succotash the next day, and who pulled the blinds against the heat at 10:00 A.M. She was also the one, she told me once, on our way up to the attic to put some quilts away in a cedar chest, called Red. My grandfather had even yelled up the stairs, "Hey Red!" She had fallen in love with the back of that man's neck, one day on a streetcar, on her way to work in 1901.

I HAD two old aunts named Edna and Grace who kept house with my grandmother along with Uncle Ed, who was also very old. Although we called them "Aunt," they were really my grandmother's nieces, but close to her in age. Aunt Edna and Aunt Grace were like moths in their summer dresses. Or weary, end-of-the-season butterflies, yellow or orange dust scattered on wings almost transparent, about to break. Their dresses were usually cut from fabric printed with nosegays, or little groups of umbrellas. It was necessary to wear a slip underneath, and on hot days, necessary to pull the drapes, get out the droning floor fan with metal blades, and take the dress off and walk around in your slip. My grandmother, otherwise very fusty and prudish, let me know this was all right, this walking around in a slip on a hot summer day.

It was not as if my aunts were like Maggie in *Cat on a Hot Tin Roof* — they were some old moths, familiar and fragile as something you might find in the attic. They offered you their cheeks for a kiss, cool and wrinkly. Aunt Grace's cheek was brisk and efficient. She was a schoolteacher who drove in a mint-green Chevy with fins to her job teaching English all the way to a high school in Granite City, Illinois. Aunt Edna's cheek was slack and receding, and smelled like a cedar chest does when you open it up after a long time. She was a maiden aunt with no job, who seemed to occupy no other role in the world, as far as I could tell, than to be a maiden aunt living in the house of my grandmother. Sometimes she shelled peas on the porch, and she played many, many games of canasta with me on long, boring, hot summer afternoons, king, queen, jack, ten, queen, jack, ten, nine, in my grandmother's living room with the drapes drawn and the floor fan droning.

Aunt Grace's culinary specialty was watermelon pickles, which were produced several times during the summer at dinner, served on a cut-glass dish, and always introduced as "Aunt Grace's watermelon pickles." She also played the endless games of canasta. You could tell that she was a woman of the working world only because there were stacks of scrap paper, in different places in the house, made out of 8 × 12 paper torn into four quarters. The backs of the papers were covered with blue print from a ditto machine; they had been grammar exercises of the tedious kind that English teachers seldom give out these days. This was as much of a profile as I could put together — peas, canasta, brisk or slack cheeks, watermelon pickles, and some old dittos. What was in their hearts? No hints were given. They were always included in family gatherings, and always stood with us for photographs, in their dresses, in those pictures taken of the whole family, in the backyard, on a very hot summer day. Aunt Grace looks forthright. Aunt Edna looks like she will soon fade into the clouds above.

My grandmother's house had four bedrooms upstairs, and she seemed glad to have one of them filled by Aunt Grace and Aunt Edna. Grandma was clearly the queen bee mother in the house and liked it that way. This seemed appropriate to me, since my grandmother had been a mother in the past — the moth aunts, however, had only been spinsters, and thus, it seemed to me, their range of experience was far too narrow to ever preside over the management of a whole household with the same stature as my grandmother. They seemed happy or at least resigned to living under my grandmother's roof, and in fact seemed deferential to her judgment on any household matter. Were the peaches ripe or not? Did the fruit and vegetable huckster come through the alley in back Wednesdays or Thursdays? How could they be expected to know, really? They had never been married or had children. Their expertise was lim-ited — watermelon pickles, not a whole roast chicken with mashed potatoes, gravy, succotash, and angel food cake. I believe they were also entrusted with the care of some brown irises in the backyard, but certainly not the entire garden.

Their bedroom was down the hall from my grandmother's. It was always very neat, with the white chenille bedspreads perfectly smoothed, and smelled faintly of lilac water and cedar closets. There were two huge bureaus and one piece of furniture we children found fascinating, a tall, dark, gloomy wardrobe that actually opened with a key — the kind of key with no notches in it and a curlicue handle on the end. It looked like the kind of key a fairy might be given in a story, to unlock something important. However, it only opened the door of the large drafty wardrobe, and inside hung more of those thin, moth-wing dresses they both wore on summer days. On the bottom were severe-looking tie oxford shoes with a small heel that we always identified as "old lady" shoes, which came in black and white. That was all. No feather boas, dried corsages, trophies, programs from the ballet, pictures of old sweethearts, rhinestone tiaras, graduation mortarboards, no moments of bygone, better, and more exciting times.

As far as I could tell, their lives, in the time that I knew them, were expected to proceed within the parameters of their role as elderly children in my grandmother's house. They would help out, but not orchestrate. The tide of their daily lives seemed to be determined by such things as how hot it was, and at what time should the shades be drawn in the living room and if a letter from Aunt Charlotte or Aunt Mabel was in the mail, and if they were running low on flour, if there were enough jokers in the canasta deck, and if there were weevils in the flour, and if the brown iris needed cutting back this year, and if the neighbor's tomatoes were ripe, and if he needed help picking them because he was color-blind, and yes, the lima beans were too starchy this time. Of course, they were old when I knew them, seventy or so.

A summer day in this household was capped off like this: Clear the dinner table, then scrape the crumbs off the tablecloth with a peculiar silver device which looked like an ornate dustpan. If jelly had fallen on the lace tablecloth, remove it immediately, before a stain set in. This nightly ritual always captured my attention with its drama. It was the efficient Aunt Grace who boiled up a pot of water with a sense of urgency. She tucked an empty pot underneath the lace cloth, and then poured boiling water from a height of three feet through the tablecloth. It was thought that the higher the fall of the water, the more effective it was. This duty done, with my grandmother in charge of the more complicated task of washing the dishes, and Uncle Ed always in charge of rolling his shirt sleeves up and drying the dishes, it was time to retire to the front porch, to sit in yellow metal chairs in the shape of fans and take in the evening air.

On a series of summer evenings in August that lasted six or seven consecutive days, Aunt Edna had been chosen to be visited by a white cabbage butterfly. The same way Aunt Edna always came out with the others, after the evening chores, to sit in the fan chair, the butterfly came to sit on Aunt Edna's arm. Her arm, perfectly still on the cool metal armrest, crisscrossed with wrinkles, but soft and still, except for the quiet pulse beneath. It was Edna who seemed the most content to live by the risings and fallings of heat and daylight, of cool air and night. No one we knew had ever been visited by a butterfly on a regular basis. Her arm was the perfect resting place for one at the end of its season.

I do not know what dreams kept them going, beyond the will to wake, eat, rest, and dream again a little at night, or what past they had left behind. It seemed to me that very little made them happy. Eventually, a few years apart from each other, they died quietly of heart attacks. Aunt Edna was first. It is hard to imagine how Aunt Grace felt that day, looking across at the other perfectly smoothed white chenille bedspread, the frugal costume jewels and trinkets on the opposite bureau, the moth dresses that didn't belong to her left in the wardrobe they shared.

ALTHOUGH he couldn't have been more than a few years younger than my grandmother, Uncle Ed was my grandmother's nephew. This did not make him my uncle in any technical sense — it was just the most convenient term. As I have said, my grandmother was the last and only child of her parents, who each had six other children from their respective previous marriages. One child from each of those marriages married each other, and had children. So, my grandmother had nieces and nephews who were very close to her own age. Aunt Grace and Aunt Edna fell into this group. The fact that he was my grandmother's nephew, and so old, and kept a room right down the hall from her, made Uncle Ed seem sort of like an old boy, once lost, but now found.

When we came for our weekly visit to Grandma's house, the routine went something like this: We met Grandma at the front door, her face anxiously emerging behind a sheer white curtain over the glass on the door (she believed every trip in a car was a brush with death). Grandma then gave us the comics she saved from the *St. Louis Globe-Democrat*, since my family was a staunch *Post-Dispatch* family. Then back to the kitchen to check on the weekly batch of cookies with the scalloped edges. Then up the back stairs from the kitchen, down the hall to the end to Uncle Ed's room. He was not the type to run downstairs to greet us, so we always went to see him. His little room was spartan — a desk, an iron bedstead, a radio, a door that led to a balcony that was too rickety to stand on. Did

Uncle Ed ever fling open those doors and stand outside to suck in the night air?

It seemed unlikely. He seemed to be a man of few and select passions. The baseball game. Shining the fins on his car with a chamois cloth. Pepper on his lima beans. A stiff martini, when he was at our house. My grandmother's house was dry. When we ran into his room, he always seemed inordinately pleased and embarrassed at the same time. Who were these children who actually liked him? On his desk, there was a pen that had a little ship floating inside, and a rock with odd striations crisscrossing it, which was reputed to be from Granite City. The radio was a desk model with a dial, perched on top of some futuresque-looking legs. It seemed to be permanently tuned to Harry Carey announcing the St. Louis Cardinals. My grandmother's house was so close to the ballpark that you could hear the tail end of a roaring crowd when there was a home run — so for an especially exciting home game, there was almost an echo between Uncle Ed's Magnavox and the sounds of the fans lifting over the streets. He had a brown-and-white plaid bedspread that seemed appropriate for a bachelor who once made a living on the Ford assembly line, or a boy, or an old boy. On a Sunday afternoon, even in the notorious summer heat of August in St. Louis, he'd be mopping his forehead with a handkerchief, but wearing a white, long-sleeved, starched shirt anyway.

Uncle Ed did not kiss us in greeting — not out of any ill will, but out of some old reluctance, some old reticence, and we accepted this deficiency as something that went along with his iron bedstead and little piece of granite from an Illinois quarry. Instead, he'd reach deep into his pants pocket and fish out a quarter for each of us — at that time, a substantial amount of money. You could consider walking up to the Woolworth's on Grand Avenue and buying anything ranging from an entire pack of rubber bands to a goldfish.

Aside from these things — pepper on lima beans, a stamp collection in his closet, a balcony that didn't work, a chamois cloth for the fins of his car, the fact that he called my grandmother Stell, the endless drone of ball games on summer afternoons, an attentive silence at the dinner table, no kisses, some other relatives who lived in Omaha, and his nightly drying of the dinner dishes — I knew very little about him. As with my aunts, it was not clear what agency, save shelter and survival, kept him alive to enjoy the small, subdued pleasures of life — night air on the porch, freshly baked bread, stewed rhubarb — in the slowly moving house of my grandmother. I knew that he had held some sort of job in the past, not worth remarking upon in the present. That his life in the past, in general, did not bear out telling now. No tales of tornadoes, floods in the Mississippi, the opening of the Fox Theatre, hopping freight cars, growing rutabagas, the first trolley line in St. Louis, war stories, Depression survival stories. This was also true of my aunts — they all seemed to be old people with no tangible past, just locked into the present moment of 1956 or '57 or '58, turning another card over on the canasta deck or taking a shiny quarter out of a pocket. They seemed to be people of no passions, no past. Or without the ability to remember them or speak them, or impress them upon a child.

Uncle Ed died silently as well — his heart, they said. He was buried in a distant city, Omaha or Des Moines. About eight years later, a thunderstorm knocked out the lights in our house. I was alone with my grandmother. My mother had been dead now for two years or so, and just that day my father had gotten married again. My grandmother, always one to try to do the right thing, had flown east from St. Louis to attend the wedding, at the age of eighty-one. At the last minute, she felt a little poorly, she said, and did not go to attend the second wedding of the man who had married her daughter twenty-seven years earlier. She stayed on in the house to see about me. When the storm knocked out the electricity, I realized I had never sat with my grandmother in the dark, in candlelight. It was a little spooky, a little nice, because for the first time, it seemed as if she needed me to sit with her as much as I needed her to sit with me.

On the night of my father's wedding, she told me the old stories, about her mother coming over on a boat from Germany when it took six weeks, and they had water and brown bread only. About her mother's four husbands, about an old farm and meeting my grandfather, about her lame knee and leaving school and peeling potatoes for fourteen brothers and sisters. "Edward," she said, "was an orphan." His mother was her half sister, killed with his father in a carriage accident. My grandmother's mother took him in when she was fifty-one, and estranged her husband in the process, who said, "Enough children." So she moved my grandmother and Uncle Ed off to a farm in Ferguson, then a community of small farms outside of St. Louis. It defies my practical or poetic imagination to see how a woman in her fifties, separated from her fourth husband, managed to scratch a living for herself and two children as well, on a farm in Ferguson in 1882.

Uncle Ed was a lost boy, and I am glad he could spend his last years quietly listening to Harry Carey and the St. Louis Cardinals, down the hall from my grandmother. He ate cornflakes with her in the morning, and they listened to the news together. That night, Grandma told me that Uncle Ed had been married for a year, once, that something had gone wrong, and it seemed to me that whatever had happened was responsible for us finding him still in his room at the end of the hall, looking a bit like a lodger in his own house, when we came to visit on Sunday afternoons.

A Solid House

"SPENDING THE NIGHT" at my grandmother's house was marked
by rituals that sent me hints of decades before my life began — the
laundry soap she learned to make out of bacon grease in the
Depression, the fading border of acanthus leaves on the wallpaper
from the 1920s. There was the stir of the Hebert Street streetcar
right outside the front window, which would soon see its last days
in service. Our own house was "modern" by comparison, built in
1948 and furnished along sleek lines, free of the Victorian of my
grandmother's house, which my mother dismissed as "ugly." So my
grandmother's house was a museum, a history book, another womb,
to be inspected deeply on the weekly basis of our visits.

No stone, no drawer, no corner, was left unturned, and each
detail seemed to invite interpretation of the times that we had not
witnessed. What kind of life was it, anyway, when you spent the
afternoon in a rocking chair overstuffed with horsehair, so that you
might get stuck with a spiky piece of hair? If there were no toys in
my grandmother's house, except for a weather-beaten hardball
downstairs, what did that imply about a childhood lived in that
house, my mother's in fact? A cheerless, toyless vision of childhood
in the 1920s opened up. My mother, sitting in a horsehair chair,
getting stuck with hairs, pensively poking an embroidery needle
back and forth through a quilt patch, sighing with boredom. My
mother, helping to fill a glass dish with rhubarb. My mother, stand-

ing on the stairs, not knowing whether she should go up or down, because that is the way I certainly felt there. It seemed as if the house were a book to be read, but that you had to supply the meaning of what you read there yourself.

My grandmother had a benign aspect, but was not demonstrative in the least. Her fresh cookies were the currencies of our exchange, the physical evidence that she was thinking of us before we even got there. She let it seem as if she just happened to have them on hand. Though it was the fifties, the era of such fabrications as Wonder bread and Oreos, my grandmother kept to the habits of earlier decades, scorned the word "store-bought," and baked her own bread and cookies on the same day every week. The butter cookies were said to be exceptional because of their extreme thinness and crispness — thick cookies were also scorned — and the bread was praised for the excellent toast it made.

I kept her wooden rolling pin. The sound of it slapping down a pastry cloth reminds me of her weekly, beautiful chore, the blending of flour and milk, butter and sugar. This ritual must have calmed the fears that attended a woman who survived lameness, poverty, the death of loved ones, for ninety-three years, by kneading and rolling out the same two perfect white foods every week. When we spent the night, she'd offer us a tin, with a photo of kittens or a poinsettia on it, filled with the fragrant cookies with scalloped edges. We ate in a kitchen that might have been on a farm in Kansas or Nebraska — roosters on the wallpaper, oilcloth on the table, a big white sink and a marble slab, a tall pantry with flour and sugar in tins, to keep out weevils. She'd lay out green cereal bowls for the next day's breakfast and tune in the radio to the CBS news. Then up the gray "kitchen" staircase to the bath.

The bath itself presented more hints about life lived in another era. Ours at home was streamlined, tiled white throughout. At my grandmother's, there was a bathtub with tall feet, the tub deep and tall, which made bathing seem a more serious affair. The spigots for the water were knobby, and you actually had to stop up the drain with a plug attached to a chain. The towels were cotton, but a little threadbare, faded, and worn. My grandmother washed and hung them again in a sensible fashion until they truly could belong to the ragbag. There was a marble slab on the sink, and a dish for the special soap — a hunk of soap that was made from little shreds of leftover soap all stuck together, one of Grandma's strict house-hold economies, which my mother practiced halfheartedly in our house. In the tub, Grandma used white Ivory soap, not the svelte pink Lux cakes my modern mother chose. The overall impression, between the claw feet, the dim light, the threadbare towels, and the plain soap, was of measured care, that life lived in this room had gone on and would go on. After being washed in that tub, I can remember feeling righteously clean in some older, deeper way, clean in the serious way that my mother, in her undoubtedly joyless childhood, must have felt, scrubbed with scraps of soap and dried with threadbare, but very clean, towels.

After the bath, we went down the long hall to bed, in the "front" room that faced onto Hebert Street and the streetcar. The room was a catchall for odd pieces of furniture and a spare bed. My grandmother's old treadle sewing machine, the one she is said to have used for a skirt for my Aunt Lois with 107 pleats once, sat between the windows. It was a source of constant, anxious specu-lation for me. Its curlicued wrought-iron bottom obviously did not belong to the 1950s, and its lack of electric connection made it seem faintly ominous, some sort of iron maiden that had bound my grandmother with her bad knee to its labor. If you opened up the lid, you saw the alarming undersides of the machine.

Looking out the windows, you were faced with more windows peering at you from the stolid row of nearly identical brick houses across the way; you were reminded of your place. There were more signs from past eras of enthusiasm. A Tiffany-style lamp, with its base in the shape of a tree, tiny acorns at the end of the chain pull. A ruler in the desk from Peveley Dairy that confidently, boldly proclaimed, "MILK — America's Greatest Food." A shiny hunk of mica, saved from a cross-country trip twenty years before, now filled up the desk's inkwell. You could sit at your own peril in the horse-hair rocker, usually accompanied by an old copy of *Reader's Digest,* the only available reading material except for *Our Daily Bread.* At least in *Reader's Digest* you could count on a story about hikers trapped under an avalanche, or a school-bus load of children stranded in a mudslide, all saved in the end, through faith and hope. These stories of disaster made the walls of her house seem stronger. The remnants of survival from past eras, the camphor-scented patch quilts, the crocheted afghans, were evidence that life's history would continue here, in a house built on decency and survival, if not generosity and celebration.

Grandma knew how to put you to bed, because she had been doing such things for seventy years now. It took a little longer to get to sleep there, because of the hiss and the lights of the streetcar outside. I fell asleep by staring at the wallpaper border of fading acanthus leaves. Eventually, the leaves assumed their place in the pattern of things, in the message of this house. Outside the streetcar wound itself out to Grand Avenue on its electric wires.

MY grandmother's house was the past and the future, surrounded by solid walls. Yet I have always had recurring dreams of its dissolution. In one dream, the house is still there, a bit elevated on its little hill, but the rest of the neighborhood has been completely razed, burned, or leveled, gone to seed in vacant lots. Or, the house is still there, but the rooms are now cut up, mismatched. Or the cabbage-rose wallpaper has been changed to red and textured or shiny wallpaper that you might find in a roadside diner. It's become a transient place. Sometimes, in a dream, the house has been deeded to me. It feels like bliss, to have this wonderful space both lived and imagined, all to myself. But then I go up to the corner to the hardware store and get lost, one wrong turn leading to another until I'm standing next to a freeway, or I've stepped on a subway to the dark heart of a foreign city by mistake, and that solid house is all gone. In another kind of dream, the house has been bought up by a fresh-faced couple who paint the somber woodwork and mantel-piece bright white, who cover the maroon-and-pink cabbage-rose wallpaper in smooth tones of peach. It seems incredible in the dream that anyone could regard these rooms without their meta-phors, without their hints of lives gone by. Oddly, this last version of the dream has come true.

A recent article in the *St. Louis Post-Dispatch* describes a boom in my grandmother's old neighborhood. The author praises the stan-dard-issue stained-glass window in the hallway, comments on the total lack of counter area in the kitchen, counts up the number of tiles in the fireplace. It shows a picture of a living room, nearly identical to the one in my grandmother's house, redone to the style of the 1990s. In front of the windows, where Aunt Edna's, Aunt Grace's, and my grandmother's favorite sitting chairs were, and also the one said to be my dead grandfather's favorite, and the couch where I once slept off a case of the measles, and the spot where the card table was pulled out for canasta, now sits a white sectional couch. In Grandma's house, this was the place where we sat rest-lessly waiting for Sunday dinner, trying to be polite and converse with someone sixty or seventy years older, where my grandmother stashed her sewing basket full of mysterious "darning eggs," in front of the windows whose shades were strictly regulated with the fluc-tuations of daily heat. White, too, is the fireplace, the one that used to be a thoughtful brown affair, carved with leaves and flowers, and tiled over with shimmery green squares. It was a gas fireplace, long since outdated. We could never figure out why we couldn't build a fire in it. The highlight of the mantelpiece used to be a marble bust of Sappho, translucent and serious. I do not think my Grandmother knew that Sappho was a poet, but simply felt that she lent an appropriately classical note to her parlor. There is also a story that my grandfather received Sappho as payment for some dental work in the Depression, and so Sappho stayed.

In the newspaper version, another white sectional couch takes the place of a table that boasted a lamp in the shape of a man who held up the lampshade. There was not much logic in its design. The title of the sculpted man was *Soldat Spartiate.* He was able to hold up the lampshade, which was made of glass, hand-painted, with blowsy roses all over it. I don't know if my grandmother really knew who the Spartan soldier and Sappho were, officially, except that they probably seemed to be a good indicator that she would never again be the girl peeling potatoes for fourteen brothers and sisters, or the girl going to work in a shirtwaist factory by streetcar.

The sectional couch also occupies the spot given over in my grandmother's living room to a very substantial Magnavox TV. It sat on its own table, and was tall and a little ominous. Years later I looked at old pictures, and found one of my sister and brother and three cousins all staring pointedly into one corner of the room. I couldn't figure out why until someone asked me what it was that was cut out from the corner of the photo — the famed Magnavox television. My grandmother's TV was tuned, it seemed, to only three shows: *Love of Life,* with its sweeping organ introduction, *Lawrence Welk,* bursting with champagne bubbles and the seven pink, maniacally smiling Lennon sisters with parasols, and *Perry Mason. Perry Mason* was the object of my endless speculation, since it came on just as I had to leave to go back to our house, or upstairs to bed, and its grinding, hit-the-pavement theme song seemed to imply everything that was mean and intriguing about adult life.

These rooms were full of ghosts for me: of my grandmother and mother, Sappho, bygone gas fires, dreamy afternoons of childhood fevers and canasta games to pass the afternoon heat. Now, in the realtor's version, this room just offered many opportunities for white-on-white. The cut glass, Sappho, and the somber mantelpiece, and all they had implied about history and permanence, were erased.

The other dreams I had about this house also came true. On a recent visit to the old neighborhood, I saw large weedy lots and crack houses. Grand Avenue was a depressed limbo-land, with transient businesses for fried fish, some pool halls, storefront churches. The Woolworth's where we bought goldfish was a boarded-up check-cashing parlor. Hebert Street had been quartered off from traffic, to encourage care of the neighborhood, and it did look a little like it was on its way back. The same eighty-year-old daffodils were blooming in the front yard. But those dreams were not just about urban change. They were about the dissolution that surrounded this solid-looking house. The members of my family, with their progressive disasters, were the leveled and smoking vacant lots. The lost trips to the corner, the alarm at finding myself so far from home, were the same as the many moments in later life when I would stop, suddenly, not having any idea about why I was standing next to some dark subway tracks in Brooklyn, or staring at a broccoli stalk in a farmhouse in New Hampshire, or walking over a train trestle in Detroit.

THE alarming element in all of these dreams was the hint that this house could be lost, or leveled. In my mind it stood as a shrine of stability. But the truth of the dream shows that it could be violated. The dream of certainty we children built around ourselves was prey to the outside. The "outside" could include urban decay, real-estate speculators, and even cut-rate wallpaper salesmen, but more deeply, included the family that must go home, from the old house with thick walls, to live in their own house. When that house is not truly a shelter, the solid-looking house presents itself as an antidote, the place of peace. We persisted in this idea because we needed a feeling of safety. You could hardly tell my brother and me now, that if we were to magically have this house again, we wouldn't be completely happy as soon as we walked through the front door. That we couldn't just walk upstairs to go see Uncle Ed again and have nothing better to do than wait until the angel food cake came out at the end of dinner. This was a place of innocence, where expectations seemed always fulfilled. Of course, this was because the expectations were so limited — we learned to expect only the brisk kisses from Aunt Grace, the sagging ones from Aunt Edna, the quarter from Uncle Ed, the box of scalloped cookies from Grandma. Further intrigue was not part of the routine. The past and the future were foreshortened, nothing like what you were waiting for in your own house. The house of limited possibility seemed the more solid of the two.

But what was the solid house for us had not been one for my mother and her sister. I do not know exactly how it happened, but I observed the results. There was the broad picture: my mother's long-standing restraint, quietness, resignation, sainthood; my aunt's terrible shyness, her feelings of being overwhelmed, eventually resulting in a damaging bout with irrationality and many, many years of near reclusion. There were the smaller, more suggestive hints of what might have been wrong in that house, though these were hard to pick up. My grandfather was said to have been a genial sort, and our grandmother was kindly and devoted to us in her restrained way. What could have been wrong? Something. My father remembered my aunt coming to open the door when he arrived to collect my mother for a date. As soon as she opened the door, she ran away, he said, like a scared rabbit.

THERE never seemed to be any cracks in my grandmother. She did things routinely, and properly. Same bread every week, same cookies, same Sunday dinner. She controlled the summer heat by making iced tea before the heat of the day struck, by pulling down the window shades, and by turning on a lazy fan with big steel blades at a particular hour. She always wore earrings and pearls, from the first moment in the morning until the last at night. There were few moments of dismay or outright joy — the strongest I can remember was the crestfallen afternoon of the crumbly bread. She might register mild pleasure when her grandchildren did something amusing in her house, like use the soup ladle hanging in the pantry as an elevator crank so we could stand in the dark pantry next to bags of flour and pretend to be ascending, further than the roof, to the clouds.

Grandma would borrow our dolls for a week or so for a "fitting" sometimes, and it was then that I glimpsed another Estella. She had trained as a "French" seamstress and drawn designs for dresses on her own. The dolls returned with black velvet coats and hats lined with silk, fluffy silk moire party dresses, pinafores in flowered crepe de chine, or flannel pajamas printed with lambs. Hand-sewn, tiny buttonholes, mother-of-pearl or rhinestone buttons, perfectly finished hems. But the comment that came back with the new set of clothes was always the same: "Oh! It was so much work!" As if the scraps of silk, the pleasure when they passed through her hands, must be turned back to straw, to duty.

I did not see her cry at my mother's death. Maybe she collected herself for me, or she was able to make her peace with this passing through Swedenborg. I equated her with the church ladies at the graveside — similarly misled, maybe demented, and finally useless, maybe hurtful in their confidence at my dead mother's "happiness," since it seemed to deny my sorrow and devastation. I thought that my grandmother's feelings were controlled in the same manner as the St. Louis heat — with routine, prescription, and duty. Her daughter's early death never seemed to be a cruel, irrational mistake to her, but just another pattern of the spheres.

Occasionally she told me something that seemed to indicate that the white-haired woman with button earrings and a fresh angel food cake had a secret life of the heart. One hint had been hearing that her nickname was Red, and that she had fallen in love with the back of a neck on a streetcar. She also confessed once that she thought she'd die when that man, her husband, died one day. The idea of her surrendering to grief and despair seemed foreign. Wouldn't she just put on a fresh dress, and some pearls, and order up some strawberries from the huckster who came through the alley, and make more jam? Wouldn't she have just gone to church on Sunday, and understood the higher purpose?

The story, however, had a restorative conclusion. After my grandfather died, she said, she was at a loss for how to continue financially. This was a bit perplexing, because my grandfather appeared to have been the solid sort, a dentist with good instincts for the stock market. But he had given away a lot of free fillings during the Depression, and some of his stock dealings were on the speculative side. He was a bit of a gambler. But my grandmother had this sewed up as well. She explained that one of his investments had been an apartment house on Queens Boulevard. Shortly after his death, the city of St. Louis had announced plans to build the four-lane Kingshighway, which was to cut right over the Queens Boulevard property. The house went, but Grandma got a substantial settlement, which set her up for a secure widowhood. She interpreted the fact that the highway was destined for her apartment house as a delib-

erate act of God. "And so you see," she said, as if narrating something as matter-of-fact as tying a shoe, "He provided for me." Even
what was askew with the man she loved, the wise-cracking dentist
with a penchant for speculation, and even his loss and his possible
neglect of her future as a widow, could be viewed as a divine act.
She once told me that although my father drank, he was a good
man, and would go to heaven. There seemed to be no end to the
ways of justifying the ways of men to her system.

I finally found a little crack in this system once, in one of the
last stories she ever told me. I had gone to spend the night with
her, in the Tower Grove Manor Apartment House. She had given
up her house on Hebert Street and chosen to live in a situation of
semidependence in a residence for older people that offered dinner
and some housekeeping support. She was in her nineties, and still
laid out the green bowls for breakfast the night before, still plunged
around her apartment with a walker and a little dustcloth, still managed to get out an old embroidered pink patch quilt when I came
to visit. So we had eaten our meal downstairs in the cafeteria, and
she had shown me off to all her friends, Ida and Isabelle and Tillie.
We joined Clara, a tiny hunchbacked woman who used to be a
teacher, for the evening news in her apartment. It was like being in
a dormitory, with its residents eating together, trading confidences,
visiting each other's rooms. It seemed a positive antidote to the
isolation of old age. We came back to her apartment. She settled
into her chair and picked up some knitting, this time long white
bandages for a leper colony.

The little ticking wind-up clock spread itself over the room, over
the couch with the claw legs and the ceramic dishes full of porcelain
flowers. There was now nothing else but the night falling outside,
onto the traffic of Grand Avenue and the Kroger supermarket parking lot next to us. My mother was dead, my father remarried, my
sister and my aunt isolated in their illnesses, my brother out of

touch with any of us. I was about twenty, in between living in a tent, or a farmhouse, or an apartment in the city, between studying painting or music or macramé or psychology, hardly the likeliest candidate for a confidence. But I was the one who was there. My grandmother was telling the story again of how Uncle Ed became an orphan, from the horse-and-buggy accident. She got to the part where her mother wanted to take them in, but her father said, "Enough children." Now she added a part.

"He was mean to her," my grandmother said, and I could tell that the thought of anyone hurting her mother still caught at her throat, some eighty years later. I thought about chickens scratching around in the yard, and potatoes being peeled as thinly as possible in 1892. "He was mean," my grandmother said again. "And you know, I never visited him, my own father, when he was dying." A little tear escaped down the side of her face, the first I had ever seen on her cheeks. "Maybe I should have," she said, and looked off someplace for a second. It was the first hole I had ever glimpsed in my grandmother's life, the first irremediable hole that was a sorrow without resolution, a sorrow without salvation, a sorrow that was all hers. And finally, a sorrow that might be mine, too, like the one about my father, whom I was not visiting. Somehow, it seemed that it would be all right to be faulted, wrong, or vicious, or small-minded, or vengeful. This moment was a gift of as much help to me as homemade bread or Swedenborg, as the Sunday comics, or a night spent in lilac-scented sheets listening to streetcars strain themselves out to the end of the line. Just that one tear, and some doubt, finally.

IT'S 1990. My mother long dead, my grandmother dead, my father dead for three or four years, my older sister dead now for three months. Official cause, a heart irregularity, manic depression, and chronic alcoholism. Unofficial cause, heartbreak. She left behind two children, now grown up. I have persuaded them to visit me, despite the difficult times. Her daughter lives in Phoenix, and flies all over the Midwest and Southwest on her job as a flight attendant. She wakes up in Chicago, or San Francisco, or Baton Rouge, all in the same week maybe. Tells me about watching pelicans, and thunderstorms, and the sadness of children, alone in airplanes, taking solo trips to visit a divorced parent on the other end. How hard those hours are for the children, and so for her, up in the air. Her son lives in Kansas City, studies biology, works all night, then stays up playing rock music. He tells me about being in many car accidents, falling asleep at the wheel, being struck and flung in the air when crossing a street. I see that my sister's illness sent her children flying, that they did not have a strong enough impression that anyone cared if they did.

I persuade them to visit me, and sleep happily, heavily, when I know they are in my house. I know I can only have them for a short time. I don't want them to leave, ever. I am hoping fervently that they think my house is solid, a place to rest. I don't want them to pick up a ripple of trouble here, and become disconsolate when they, smart alley cats alert to changes in the weather, do anyway. I want to be that solid thing that I cannot be quite yet. I want to be my idea of my grandmother, in a big Victorian house, with a room for each of them, with a reliable set of sighs and pearls, even a daily soap opera, and set out making them succotash from the leftover corn. I want to keep them. I want them to come home. For the first time, I seem to know what my grandmother was doing, filling those glass dishes with rhubarb, playing canasta with the moth aunts, her aged nieces, ironing a shirt for Uncle Ed, her orphan nephew of the horse-and-buggy accident. She was holding on.

Sassafras, Sumac

MY old aunts, Edna and Grace, and my grandmother were all coming out to the house on a weekday. This didn't happen often. We usually went to their house on Hebert Street for the regulation Sunday dinner. It was the end of summer, a ninety-eight-degree kind of day pressing down on us. The aunts and Grandma would be wearing their thin weekday "wash" dresses. We were making jelly, an occasion that required all the extra hands you could get, even the elderly hands of Grace, Edna, and Estella. This yearly event always thrilled me because of all the noise and activity, but also because it fed into one of my primary fantasies: that although I had come from city people, I was born to live on another plane of existence. I was meant to be on a farm, born to sit in hay and talk to animals, the way Fern did in *Charlotte's Web*. The presence of a brushy field behind our house, which was really only an under-developed tract of land between our house and the highway, about a half-mile wide, supported my belief. In my eyes, it was a complex world, variegated with gullies, a tiny stream that depended on the rainfall for its appearance, twisty and enigmatic paths through the weeds, special groves of cottonwood and persimmon trees, a hilly spot with unreliable footing where blackberries grew, the oak that stood like a monument at the top of the hill. All of this would one day become a bland brick apartment complex — overnight, it seemed.

But at the time, the combination of reading about the barnyard conversations of geese, pigs, and sheep in *Charlotte's Web,* examining the asters embroidered on my patchwork quilt, knowing Missouri was close to Dorothy's Kansas, reading *Little House on the Prairie,* looking out my bedroom window to fields with weeds my father could name, sassafras, sumac, was enough to convince me that I was practically on my way to the state fair to win a prize for a pig or a pie. And the fact that my father, brother, and I took the collie dog out to this field, and let the dog off his leash to lead us to the best berry patch, as he gathered clumps of burrs in his fur, which we would later have to comb out, only convinced me further that I was meant to be a gatherer of my own food, that someday I would hold armfuls of my own wheat. So when my aunts arrived to make jelly, from the berries picked and gathered from the hands of my own family, it seemed that we were now traveling toward my past glorious life, wild in the field, or my future glorious life, walking my pig to Kansas, walking my wheat to the Enterprise Flour Mill.

Jelly making was the most complicated cooking procedure I had ever witnessed. It seemed to be a cross between what I thought of as life-in-the-olden-times and a chemistry experiment. The largest aluminum pots were hauled out. Then came a cooking thermometer with a jumpy needle. There were clouds of rising steam, troublesome in the ninety-eight-degree day. "Mason" jars, a name I always confused with the mysterious order of the Masonic Temple that one of my grandfathers had belonged to, were brought from the basement, sterilized in oversized pots of boiling water, and set to dry by the window. You were cautioned not to touch them, because of the "germs." The berries were washed, drained, measured; the proportionate amount of sugar was looked up in *The Joy of Cooking* and added; then the berries were boiled, the temperature checked.

Some members of the family accepted jam with seeds. Others prized clear jelly, without seeds. For jelly, the berries, once boiled, were strained through a linen cloth. This is where Aunt Grace and Edna came in. Someone had to hold the linen while someone else poured from the pot. And someone had to keep an eye on the paraffin, melting slowly on the side of the stove in a small pot, since we were told it could burst into flame at any moment. The jam or jelly was too thin if you cooked it too little, and gelatinous if you cooked it too long. A germy spot anywhere inside the jar ruined the whole process. If the paraffin seal was incomplete and let air in, the jelly couldn't be stored on the shelf.

In the hot weather and clouds of steam, Aunt Edna's upper lip had a little mustache of sweat (known only as perspiration in our house). So did mine. It was in the family, they said. Aunt Grace was tall, and took up a lot of room in our kitchen. She was very efficient in holding up the linen straining cloth. After all the excitement was over, my mother would have lunch for them, a "lady's" kind of sandwich, egg salad on white toast and a tall glass of iced tea that had been brewed around six in the morning. They would eat on the back porch, on top of a "summer" tablecloth, printed with reclining Mexicans in sombreros or with bunches of cherries. They might listen to CBS News on the radio, their favorite program. Then they would admire the rows of translucent jelly, sitting by the windowsill on white tiles, all of them lit from within by the sun of an August afternoon. A few worries: was it too thick or too thin? Any of the seals broken? But the year's work was now done. Blackberries only once a year. They would later take a piece of adhesive tape for a label on the jar, and write the name of the jelly, in their obedient, correct-looking, scrawly handwriting. The beautiful names. Blackberry. Quince. Strawberry. Pear. Peach. The jars would line shelves in the basement, next to the Ping-Pong table and the squashed water bugs. We never bought jelly from a store, and I came to believe that to do so would imply a coming-down. It was exciting to be sent to the basement in midwinter to get a new jar when the old one ran out.

It wasn't really necessary to make your own jelly — or bread — in 1959. These were modern times. The Depression was over. The war and rationing were over. We didn't really live on a farm. It was a lot of trouble. You could just buy it at the store. But there was an important connection to be made here. When the huckster came to sell strawberries in the alley behind my grandmother's house on Hebert Street, she always bought from him, not "supermarket fruit." His was straight from the country, she said, and the berries went right to her marble drainboard next to the sink, to be hulled. It was the same with making jelly. We were city people, but needed to feel that we still had our hands, every now and then, in the field we left behind.

Good Mothers,
Bad Daughters

READING "Sleeping Beauty" one night to my own daughter, I was stunned to recognize my own mother's face in the picture of the thirteenth fairy — the scowly one, the one the other fairies forgot to invite to the party. Suddenly my mother's sighs and resignation and the occasional cross look, the thirteenth-fairy look, crossing over her face took on new meaning.

When I was a child, my mother appeared to me to be the same as the mother in the Dick and Jane readers. This woman decorated pastel birthday cakes, produced new kittens from her apron pockets for surprises, and sat on lawn chairs with her ankles crossed. She set up lunches for her children on card tables under shady maple trees, she put pennies in their coin purses, she held her children's hands on little trips to the bakery or the pet store. She wore Orlon sweaters, skirts, and pumps and sat next to the father for family outings in the car.

My mother provided correct-looking activities and birthday cakes for her children. She seemed benign, at least, if not radiant or even happy or even content. It wasn't until twenty or more years later that I understood that this pastel mother had a darker side. I know now that she was trying very hard to appear benign, because she thought she should, or perhaps because nothing else seemed possible — not the stories she planned to write, not the teaching job she had trained for. Somehow, by the time she was my mother, the elements of her life were quarrels with the butcher, a mostly absent husband, three children, a clean house, many wishes, and an occasional jar of fresh raspberry jelly held up to the sunlight to admire its color.

My mother died when I was eleven, so I cannot check with her about her feelings then, how she felt about being a wife and mother in the manner of the white middle class of the 1950s. She never said, outright, whether she wanted the same thing or something else for her daughters. But it always seemed as if something else was called for. My sister was older than me by almost ten years. Her response to my mother's limited portrait of the future for girls seemed to be to raise the ante of my mother's domestic heroine-hood into outright martyrdom: she would marry very young and have six children, she would convert to Catholicism, she would take a night-school course in cake decorating, she would marry a poor but brilliant man, she would make brilliant stew from chicken backs, she would look just like Kim Novak. I took the opposite track in my dreams: I would be a fireman, a cowboy, a doctor, anything clearly unlike a mother. I became a writer, a poet, a scholar, a professor, and a mother. I became the bad daughter of a good mother. But I am coming to believe that she wanted it that way, that many good mothers subverted their own culture in messages to their daughters, who would become the "bad" girls of the 1960s and beyond.

My mother seemed to behave like any other mother. She wore her hair curled away from her face, red lipstick, shirtwaist dresses, straight skirts, and V-neck blouses. Usually some kind of button-shaped earrings, white gloves in warm weather, and two-toned shoes. Pants were a rarity. Even when outdoors, she assumed a decorative posture, like the mothers in the school readers. If the family went fishing, she would not fish, but instead sat carefully in the brush, legs cast to the side in her skirt, writing letters on thin, watery-blue paper. She wrote to her sister in Iowa and to her aunt in California, with stories not about herself, but about her children.

When she went swimming, it was only for a "dip," and then in an absurd bathing cap that had fake bangs attached to it. Apparently, it was necessary to look pleasantly coiffed even when swimming. Once she was in, her arms looked like the fronds of palm or fern cutting quietly through the water — hers was a quiet sidestroke, nothing to do with kicking, thrashing, or splashing. Her house was almost barren in its neatness. There were no signs of disheveled books or newspapers, no crumbs from newly baked bread, no muddy shoes, no leaves the dog dragged in, no toys in the wake of children. I am not sure where these things were hidden. She cooked the food other mothers seemed to: chicken à la king, meat loaf, pancakes, tuna fish sandwiches improved with pickle juice, angel food cake. Our clothes were clean and ironed. There were orange flowers dutifully planted in spots around the yard, but no riotous garden.

As in every other family I know of, my father was the household king. The unspoken rule which everyone understood was that he made the money, so he set the tone. All else followed from that — how bouncy or not we were in the house, whether we told any of our own stories at the dinner table, whether my mother had any success in pouring out her heart to him at midnight. Perhaps partly because of my father's leading role in this scenario, I could not tell you to this day much about my mother's likes and dislikes, about her passions, except for odd hints.

Every day she found her way to the piano — a cavernous old Chickering baby grand, which she had somehow squeezed into the demure proportions of a suburban brick house built in 1946. I only recently realized that everything she played had the tone and tempo of melancholy, even the folk songs and children's songs she played for us. The ones she picked for herself were full of loss. The refrain of longing was the same, whether the songs were American like

"Shenandoah" — "I long to hear you / Away I'm bound to go, / 'Cross the wide [pause] Missouri" — or Eastern European love songs with doleful titles like "Bloom, My Little Bud of Rosemary." In her restrained and slightly too-slow rendition, even children's songs seemed tragic: "Go tell Aunt Lucy / Go tell Aunt Lu — u — cy / The old gray goose is dead." The plight of the three kittens who lost their mittens indeed seemed something of a lament. She was drawn to the piano at almost the same hour of every afternoon, and it was at these times that she seemed to get the closest to saying what was on her mind. But it was only close, an approximation, her song without words, which we noted the way you would note an afternoon sky changing to slate, or the color of moss.

I am ashamed to say that it seemed as if my mother were mainly another feature of the house, not any sort of passionate human being. She was the aproned person who went with the little brick house painted cool green and yellow, with primrose chintz curtains, white tiles in the kitchen, and two-toned linoleum. I see now that this one-dimensional perspective of her was not only because of my child's-eye view, that I was the center of the universe and my mother was there to serve me. It was also because my mother did not know how to name or speak her needs and desires, large or small. I do not really know if she felt most alive in a sooty city street or a woody ravine, yearned only for solitude or for a circle of admirers, liked chocolate definitely more than marzipan, would have died to be a ballerina or a brain surgeon. It seemed that the duty of mothers was not to have any desires, lost or fulfilled or not. Without desire, they were "good" mothers. This is what my mother strove to be, and it was what she was said to be.

However, it was known in our family that my mother had some unmet vocation — this strain was like a chronic illness — that she had some calling totally unrelated to making egg salad sandwiches. She had managed to graduate from college in the middle of the

Depression at the young age of twenty. She went to Washington University, during the same years that Tennessee Williams came and left, but did not know this until later. After college she worked on the *St. Louis Star-Ledger,* in a secretarial job for an editor which included writing obituaries and checking the comic strips for continuity. She had trained to be an elementary-school teacher, but, according to my father, felt too ill at ease to stand up in front of a classroom. After marriage, she worked for a couple of years at the paper, and then gave it up.

My father had had to skip college, and the fact that he had a "college-educated" wife meant that he had to be vigilant in maintaining his position as the head of the house. He was always happy to tell the story about coming home one night from work and finding my mother at the kitchen table. The table was covered with little slips of paper and an opened copy of *The Joy of Cooking.* My mother had her head in her hands. She had tried to convert the fractions in a recipe for pot roast, and somehow, even with her college degree, the "poor dear" hadn't been able to manage it. "Well," he'd say, looking happy, "I pulled out my slide rule and had the matter settled in a minute or two." Apparently this endeared her to him. At the same time, this kind of moment in married life was corrosive — and eventually helped to make the idea of her other calling more and more faraway, more like an old sigh.

The refrain of my mother's longing joins in my memory with an image of her lying on the couch for an afternoon nap. Her pumps were tossed off, and she had curled herself around a bit. This was a private retreat where we clearly were not welcome. I think that sometimes, before she went off to this solitary place, before I went back to my room to play like a good child with bride dolls and puzzles in the shape of the United States, she told me a thing or two. She became slightly confidential, the way children do before they fall off to sleep. She might say something about wanting to go back to school or wanting to write some stories. Then she took a nap. For what was the good mother of the 1950s supposed to do about dreams, desires? Mine slept on them, the way the cat slept curled on the doorstep, daily. But she did tell her daughter about them first.

Despite her determination to look and act like the women in the Dick and Jane schoolbooks, I believe that my mother wanted to save something wild in me. Direct statement was beyond her — she'd be stepping too far out of role. Dick and Jane's mother did not lament the good old days at the newspaper office, or sigh about the book she wanted to write, or tell her daughters to forget about marriage. But my mother did forbid me to read fairy tales where they cut off a dancing girl's feet, or turned ambitious mermaids to sea foam. She stopped me from joining my friends in the race to become beauty queens and little mommies. She took me on a trip four-hundred miles from our house, to visit a woman who lived with books, not children. I think many of us must have such stories — moments when our mothers, seemingly frozen in the posture of silence, broke out, briefly, to tell us about some other life they hoped for. For themselves, or for us, or for some other woman, sometime.

IT seems now that a very large amount of childhood time ticked away in the middle of the living-room floor — practicing cartwheels, waiting for Annette Funicello and the other Mousketeers to emerge from the little black dots on the TV screen, waiting for dinner, waiting for my father to read me the comics, waiting for my mother to finish paying bills, waiting to learn how to read, waiting until it was dark and the lightning bugs would come out.

One Sunday, after Sunday school and before Sunday dinner, I wore a pair of black patent-leather shoes with white anklet socks.

The shoes had a strap across the top that buckled, Mary Jane–style. The strap was "convertible" — attached to both sides of the shoe with a little hinge so you could flip it back behind your heel. What I wanted, absolutely more than anything else in life, was to be able to wear this strap in back, not over the top of my foot. That way they would look like "flats," a much more grown-up shoe than a Mary Jane.

If my shoes looked like flats, it would prove that I was grown-up, not just a child, and a girl, but a real girl like my teenage sister, who had hair spray and flats, and boyfriends with saddle shoes and cars with fins. From this shoe, the progression from childhood to full womanhood was clearly mapped out — Mary Janes to flats to pumps with a small tasteful heel, and finally to the realm of pure sex and authority, "spike" heels. We revered the sound high heels made clicking down a hallway, and vaguely knew that they also had something to do with men falling over their feet, for women. Some of the other girls in my Sunday-school class had been allowed to fix their shoes so that they looked like flats. As soon as they did this, they seemed to gain years in world-experience and expertise. I didn't think about the fact that their shoes would fall off their feet when they ran or jumped. I only thought of how sleek their feet looked, freed from childhood.

So standing in the middle of the living room, probably waiting for my grandmother to arrive carrying a basket of mending so she could keep busy waiting for Sunday dinner, I experimented with slinging the straps back. I admired the unbroken expanse of white sock. Without the strap, I felt instantly transformed, now a sinful Cinderella with some new shoes of big-girl life. I slid up and down the rug on the smooth soles of my shoes. I tried kicking them off effortlessly, the way June Allyson or Doris Day might have with their beautiful high-heeled shoes, and slipping them on again.

Somewhere in the middle of this reverie I must have run into the kitchen and asked my mother if I could now wear my shoes the convertible way all the time. All the other girls were, I'm sure I told her. No, she said quietly, you're not old enough. But Mom, I said. No, she said, you're not old enough for that, there's plenty of time for *that*. My ears burned with rage. Right then, I understood *that* to mean the whole journey to full-grown woman, from flats to pumps to high heels. To boyfriends to wedding cakes and babies crying. Something in her tone clearly meant that all of *that* was not all it was cooked up to be. Not worth sacrificing one moment of your native girlhood for, not worth changing the straps on your Mary Jane shoes.

MY mother had an old friend. This in itself surprised me, since my mother seemed to me to have little history aside from taking me to parks and frying up bacon. Her friend's name was Hope West, which I knew from seeing it on the binding of one of the books in our house. She was an anthropologist, and she and my mother had been in college together at Washington University. In August of 1959, when I was seven, my family took a short trip to Chicago, to visit the Field Museum, to have lunch in the Marshall Field's tearoom, and to visit Hope West. In the museum I was thrilled by displays of Kodiak bears, hunks of alabaster and chrysolite, and dinosaur bones. My other main concern on this trip was eating fried chicken as often as possible.

It seemed a little dreary to visit one of my mother's friends in the middle of all of this, and the August heat was thick. All of her "old college friends" I had met so far seemed to fall into one not very interesting category. They had given up their jobs, married, and had children. They had "luncheon," not lunch, with card parties once or twice a year, on card tables in their living rooms, were all very pleasant, and all seemed to be named Mary Helen or Helen

Louise. But this old friend had no children, I was told, was not married, and worked as a writer. Never had I met a woman like this.

Further, she lived by herself in an apartment. In my limited experience as a girl growing up outside St. Louis in a suburban house with a scrubby field behind it, an apartment in the city seemed to be a shrine to one's own mind. Especially this woman's apartment, since she was the author of books. As far as I knew, she and my mother hadn't seen each other since college, and now it was more than twenty-five years later.

So I knew, when we walked into her apartment at the end of a humid August afternoon, that some kind of moment had arrived for my mother. Our family — my sister, my brother, my mother and father, and myself — were much too large for Hope West's apartment. We were a bulky group that disturbed the streamlined serenity of this "modern" 1950s brick skyscraper. My parents tried to make us look spotless and presentable, dabbing at our collars or the corners of our mouths, catching stray strands of hair. But here was a seven-year-old with legs long like a young horse's, with scabby knees from falling in blackberry patches. A fourteen-year-old boy in wilted khaki pants, whose voice was changing, and who was obsessed with meteorology. And a sixteen-year-old girl with three or four crinoline petticoats and upswept blond hair so that she could look like Kim Novak in *Picnic*.

My father stood slightly aside in shirt sleeves because of the heat, and smoked a Pall Mall. His social bearing was a bit confused because this woman was a scholar and a writer. He didn't seem to know whether to adopt the polite, deferential mode reserved for elderly maiden aunts, or the more bossy, commandeering mode used with business friends. And there was my mother, a *mother* with white gloves, responsible for all of these children who were now either bumping into coffee tables, in danger of breaking the African artifacts, or rudely staring out the window at Lake Michigan. But I

remember thinking, despite our gangliness, that Hope West was
certainly the one to be pitied. She was "a woman without children" — a fate always presented in our family as a lifetime tragedy,
a sadness to be avoided at any cost.

Yet, Hope West did not look sad. She did not look like any of
the other women I had ever met, the mothers with comfortable
tummies, generous upper arms, curly hair with a little breeze in it,
wearing a print dress that puffed out at the waist. Mothers who
actually spent time crisscrossing the prongs of a fork on top of
cookies for decoration. Hope West was tall and wore a tubular
green suit. Her whole face gathered toward her hair, which was
pulled up in a French twist. Her face and her hair seemed to collect
what she was seeing and thinking.

There were no cookies waiting for us on the coffee table. One
side of the living room held a wall of books, more than I had ever
seen in anyone's house. Most important, most amazing to me, was
that all of these books were hers. On another side of the room was
a huge picture window that overlooked Lake Michigan and the tops
of buildings. Not flowers and a swing set. No one but Hope West
enjoyed this view of Lake Michigan's endless blue tabletop — hard
to imagine, when the five of us crowded around the kitchen window
at our house to look at rabbits or possums traveling through the
backyard. Her own view, and her own books — and some of them
were undoubtedly hers, of her own writing. How would it feel, I
wondered, to have your own book on your own bookshelf? Her
bookshelves, her room, her Lake Michigan. I had never met a woman
who didn't share everything with everyone. Who didn't have to give
up the best pork chop for the father or the children, who had more
than a few private things in a bureau drawer that her children always
raided. Hope West seemed strange and monumental, standing straight
and gray-eyed in her French twist, in front of her books and a long
vista outside.

Suddenly, the seemingly inevitable and unfortunate outlines of women's destinies fell into relief for me. You could be Hope West, alone, with your books, with no children. Or you could be my mother with children, and no book of your own. I felt that each of the old friends looked at the other and saw what she did not have. It seemed that I had to choose sides, then and there. Of course I thought, maybe in loyalty, that I would be like my mother, the one with children. But I had always wanted to write a book, to hold a book of my own in my hand. Did I have to choose?

We took Hope West out to dinner with us. I ate fried chicken again, and wondered what Hope West did for dinner, alone, on all those other nights, when we weren't there to take her out. My mother never did become Hope West, the writer of books, the mother of no children. But she did bring her impressionable children across four-hundred flat miles of Missouri and Illinois to visit her on an impossibly hot summer day in 1959.

HOW far could a woman walk? This question seemed to underlie another of my mother's rather odd strictures, besides the one about grown-up girl shoes. My mother was not one to forbid or censor very much. She had read Dr. Spock, after all, and was determined to be different from her mother, who was said to have been "severe." But she had been strong on the subject of those patent-leather shoes, and she was also very clear about not reading two particular fairy tales to me. This was puzzling. She believed in reading, and let me go through everything else in the house from *Mr. Dog* to photo essays on Czechoslovakia to *The Hunchback of Notre Dame.*

But there was a certain book with a languorous picture of a mermaid on the cover that I coveted. The book had a special mystique because it had belonged to my mother as a child, and because she had forbidden me to read two of the stories inside. It was a beginning-to-fall-apart edition of Andersen's fairy tales, from the

1920s, a "Washington Square Classic." The quality of the paper seemed to be just a cut above newsprint. There were only six color illustrations — the Snow Queen, Elise with the swans, a sleeping woman among water lilies, an angel with a child, the little mermaid, and a prince finding a sleeping princess in the garden of paradise. There were also two dozen other tales the illustrator could have chosen from, but he picked opportunities to paint mournful women. They were all long-haired, entwined in swans or water, and doomed.

I treasured this book because it was one of the few things my mother had kept from her own childhood. There were no favorite dolls, toys, or sweaters — just a few books. When she first brought the fairy-tale book up to my room — she must have kept it in some special part of the house, since I had never seen it with the other books — I was impressed by its age. Its yellow cover fell into the yellow light of my bedside lamp as dusk fell outside. It proved that my mother had been a child — and the fact that there were only six illustrations in a volume of so many stories further convinced me that life in the old days, my mother's old days, was deprived and strange indeed. I've carried this book with me through more than fifteen changes of address since I left home twenty years ago, carefully packing it, dusting it, yet sometimes ignoring it, letting its binding fall off. And thinking, so what if I finally lose it, knowing I would never forgive myself if I did.

Now this book brings back the feeling of what it was like in a Missouri bedroom with a view of a field of brush to be a child who thought she was safe. In flannel pajamas on ironed cotton sheets, with a wool blanket, a quilt embroidered by my aunts and grandmother that seemed to have purple asters blowing slightly in the wind, a chenille bedspread with peach and blue tufts, an oak table and chair next to the bed, and a mother who was probably even wearing a damp apron. You could pick up a little something about her when she read out loud. She did not read dramatically, or very humorously, even when it came to the burlesque parts of "The Three Bears" — but she read with feeling and thoughtfulness, the way she played the piano. You could hear more of the longing. It seemed as if she liked to be lost in the stories as much as her children did. Maybe she was a little sad, too. There was a lulling note in her voice, as if acknowledging that this story was something she could bring you for only a very short time of your life, this short time before you fell asleep and grew up.

We read all of the stories in the Hans Christian Andersen except two, "The Little Mermaid" and "The Red Shoes." I wanted to hear about them, but my mother said, "Don't read those stories. They're too sad." This was unusual for her — she made few direct statements and gave little forceful advice. So this directive coming from her stunned me. Besides, the best picture in the whole book, the cover picture even, was of the mermaid. She sat in profile, with her hair fanning out into seaweed, posed with her tail curled improbably under her at the bottom of the sea. She was so beautiful. But my mother would not read her story, in that golden light with the dusk falling outside.

Since they were forbidden, I wanted to read those stories all the more. My mother eventually gave in and read them to me. I found out that the little mermaid fell in love with a human prince, wanted to be human, and sold her tongue to a witch in order to have legs, like a princess. She got her legs, but they were a bad fit. My mother could barely choke out the line about the mermaid's legs: *they hurt like knives* whenever she walked.

It seemed to me that my mother, that many other women, who had ambitions that seemed as farfetched and unlikely as a mermaid having legs, if they wanted to roam, be a traveling writer or pursue some idea of their own making anywhere, were punished in the same way for their dreams. Maybe my mother had tried something like this once, but her *legs hurt like knives*. Why was the price for endeavor so dear? Why did the mermaid have to lose her voice, her tongue, just to be able to walk the same landscape as the prince? Another woman helped her toward what she wanted, but there was the terrible price of pain and silence. Was this helping woman a witch, a mother? Was this story just about growing up, a warning against trying to walk like a man? Or about making yourself fit for a man by becoming mute?

For all her terrible sacrifices, the mermaid fails to meet her prince. She struggles across the land in her bad legs, only in time to see, from afar, his wedding to a real princess taking place. She cannot even call out, since her voice is gone. This was more bad news for girls like me, the ones that might try to transform themselves into something else, to ask a witch, or a mother, sometime, for traveling legs. It implied that the real princess, the natural girl, the one who was born to this station, did not have to change herself. The princesses would marry the princes no matter what.

My mother was warning me that her own story and the story of my life to come might be "too sad." Would my legs turn to knives when I tried to walk? Would growing up like a girl cut my tongue out? Perhaps she thought in some primitive way that if I never read the story, none of this would happen to me. But I can tell you that for many years of my early childhood, I was awakened from sleep a few times every week by pains in my legs. I was told that they were called "growing" pains.

In the second story my mother wouldn't read, "The Red Shoes," a girl longs for a special pair of shoes. She gets them. She dances joyfully in the town square. But then her feet won't stop dancing. She's about to die from never stopping. A woodcutter cuts her feet off so that she can stop. So she stops, but she dies. It seemed to me that there was a special fate that this girl had really wanted with those red shoes. Wear red shoes. Dance and dance. But somehow this red desire for a girl was sickness. Desire will kill you eventually.

You'll be cut off at the feet by some man, sooner or later.

The mermaid, too, was cut off by desire. When she finally glimpsed the prince from far off, and could not call out on her bad legs, she became so sad that she turned to sea foam. My mother made no instructive comments about my future, like get a job before a man, be a mother or not, forget marriage. This was years before the women's movement, before women looked twice at what happened to women in the stories handed down to us. But I do know, from the way she read these stories to me, in a bedroom in Missouri in 1959, that she did not want me, her daughter, ever to walk on legs that hurt like knives, to have my feet cut off if I tried to dance, or to have my life amount to sea foam.

Away, You Rolling River

AS a very young child, I solved the problem of falling asleep at night by inventing the white horse. He fit into the palm of my hand, but when I took him out at night, and set him on the chenille rug next to my bed, he grew. Large enough, that is, to fill the space between my bed and dresser, a horse on the scale of the Clydesdales at Anheuser-Busch. Under the white horse's large and protective influence, I always fell asleep. I woke to a small framed picture of a strange, stark little landscape, a lone tree on a hillside, with dark limbs, no leaves. Outside the side window, the constant profile of daily life: a car crunching in the neighbor's driveway, a leafy cottonwood tree, a dog standing on top of his doghouse barking, the tail of a street, the hollow sound of tires on wet pavement. The other window offered a view that seemed limitless, like the stories I heard before I went to sleep. It looked out to the brush field beyond, full of sumac and blackberries, milkweed and tall grass, full of little paths, streets and cities of weeds. It rose to a hill. At its top, a handsome, perfectly rounded old oak tree guarded the field. When you were up close, its roots seemed to mark the route to the center of the earth, or to China. All the paths in the field led up to it. If you were lost, you'd follow one of the paths, and would arrive at the oak. From the oak, you could always find your way back to the house. The oak was a constant that never goofed you up with wrong directions, the true sovereign that forgave the errors of your childish wanderings, your distractions and bad sense of direction. It was the tree that could have been your father or your mother. From my window, the oak tree marked the top of the horizon, and when it was without leaves, I thought it must be the same tree as the one in the picture hanging on my wall. I looked from my bed to the tree in the picture to the tree in the field, and this was my compass. I checked the field when I woke up to make sure the oak tree was out there, the north star of a landlocked life in a flat place.

In the morning, our small brick house seemed bathed in white and yellow light, radiant. When my mother came down to get my breakfast, she was always uniformly pleasantly dressed, an ironed blouse and skirt, and pumps. She made me a small meal, a bowl of Cheerios, some French toast or pancakes, a boiled egg in a cup. We sat in the "breakfast bar," a countertop of yellow Formica surrounded by white tiles, facing a window to the backyard and the field beyond. We sat side by side, looking out to the trees and the brush. To check if the gully behind, which held water after a rainfall, had been filled up, or dried out, or washed out by a gully-washer, a really big rain. To make sure the nasty boys in the neighborhood, who hunted for rabbits with sticks, and carried bags, weren't out there. To see how deep the red in the throats of the sumac berries was. To guess if the persimmons that fell there from tall trees were ripe yet, the ones only my father could find, which he said were best eaten after one frost. To check if the possum that lay supposedly dead in the backyard was still there in the morning.

ABOUT a week after Christmas, when our tree was drying up, my mother had us spread peanut butter on bread, cut it up into cubes, and decorate the old tree with them. Then we took it outside, laid it against some shrubs in the back, and watched from the kitchen window, our elbows on the breakfast bar, waiting, while juncos, cardinals, blue jays, and other wintering birds slowly realized that a gift had been laid out for them. The red and gray and blue birds, against the white backdrop of snow, were the gifts my mother laid out for us.

My parents were determined that we would have the right kind of childhood, and daily, there were many gifts. A view of a field. A clean peach bookcase to hold treasures. A pancake in the shape of a rabbit. A sausage brought in a suitcase from Milwaukee. A table, with some paint in muffin tins, and paper. A turtle, rescued from the yard, brought into the house in a cardboard box, to live with us overnight, so we could have the privilege of feeding it lettuce leaves. Dinner, with grown-ups, with real china, a placemat, my own place at the deeply polished mahogany table. An old peanut butter jar, holes hammered in the lid, full of fireflies that spent the night in your room. A screened-in back porch, a floor above the backyard, with straw mats and blinds, where we played long games of Monopoly, and sometimes were allowed to sleep, just to enjoy the sound of late-summer cicadas. Maybe an owl, and moonlight.

I would have told you that I was a happy child. A completely happy child, though there was a constant undertone of worry. At the same time as all these gifts were spread in front of us, there were the facts of daily life. That my mother had sighed herself somewhere into the walls of the house, that my father couldn't stop looking over my brother's shoulder. That my sister was smart and pretty, and moody, and maybe a little dangerous with her arched eyebrows. That my father would crack the ice tray, and hold a martini, and be "away, 'cross the wide Missouri" even when he was there, or away on a train, crossing a long Midwestern state. Sometimes, at moments, he was clearly there, if he was fixing a faucet or picking blackberries with you. But a traveling man always has another destination.

I didn't think about these things. I knew them. They were just the themes of daily life, which I assumed every household had. You lived with them, and ate another bowl of Cheerios. Fed the dog an old marrow bone. Looked at sun on the sidewalk. Occasionally, the recurring themes emerged into a high-relief drama. The cyclical one was the arrival of my brother's report cards, which gathered all the problems of our house into the eye of one storm. Never good enough, always a source of disappointment to my father, himself the disappointed boy, now reproaching and berating himself, in the form of his small son.

Sometimes, my mother raised her voice, insisted my father not be so hard on this boy. My sister and I were the guilty girls with the straight A's, told not to sound off too much because it would make everyone feel bad. We felt guilty, all of us, but it seemed we had no real say, because my father was the one who went out and suffered the world to make money for us, so we could eat breakfast in peace and look out over our field for animals. Perhaps we felt very guilty, taking those gifts, that were not meant to be gifts but just the things of daily life.

I WISH that the very difficult job of caring for young children in isolation hadn't fallen solely to my mother, whose dreams often ran elsewhere. People believed at this time that the work of children and house belonged exclusively to the mothers, but that does not mean every mother was well suited to the job. For some, like my mother, it seemed to be a bad fit. Yet she spent a great deal of time convincing herself that it was a good fit, pinning up her daughter's hemlines, parting her son's hair, choosing ivy-patterned wallpaper for the dining room, changing the proportions in a recipe. None of this was truly absorbing, but she seemed to doggedly pursue the idea that it would be. More absorbing were thoughts about coffee in Paris, fields of wheat on the Great Plains, the color of poppies after rain in California.

She had married a man who created himself from a cold-water flat and a pack of cigarettes in the Depression. A kind of miracle. He liked ballet, he traveled around the world, was inspired by a TVA dam in Tennessee, was kind to animals, was hungry to read. He called her his best friend, when they sat together peaceably reading *The New Yorker* and the *Post-Dispatch* on an average St. Louis Saturday morning, before the children were up. He invented machines that were a little whimsical and useful at the same time. One put labels on beer bottles, another put caps on bottles of orange soda and Coke. Once, going into their bedroom early in the morning, I thought I saw them holding hands in their sleep. Their hands rested over the gap in their twin beds pushed side by side. My mother's watch with the gold mesh band leaned to the side of her wrist, fixing this small embrace at 6:00 A.M. At that moment, all seemed well with the world, and with our solid brick house.

ALL this, but he was a drinking man too. I am sure my mother knew this part of the story was eating the heart out of her family. Of course, I like to fantasize now that she could have said to him one night, "Bill, my love, you are killing yourself, killing all of us. Give it up now, or we are going." And resolutely packed her bags, our bags, moved up to one of the fake-Tudor apartment buildings on Lucas and Hunt Road. And without fear or worry about what her mother would say, called up the man she used to work for at the newspaper and asked for her old job back. We would have lived together, on a happy shoestring, with our serene single working mother of the 1950s, out from under the cloud of a moody father. Our whole house was orchestrated to avoid knowing what was troubling the businessman-with-briefcase, as if we were afraid to discover the skinny boy inside. So we held up our father, in order to eat on our mahogany table with the claw-foot legs, and sleep in our beds with quilts over our heads.

Maybe without my father to placate, to fuss at when he came through the door at night, to look the other way for, to puff up with confidence, my mother would have had more of her life for herself. More left over for the hearts and minds of her children. As it was, I have no memory of her sitting on the floor playing, or throwing her arms around me when I came home. Or drawing me into her lap, except once or twice, when I had lost a place on the other girls' softball team. She did show love in other ways — making a birthday cake, driving me downtown to ballet with the Russian madame in pink tights and white hair, choosing a book for me in the library about little girls on a walk through Paris, so that I could be a girl on a walk through Paris. Setting me out with my own paints on the back porch. Letting me be free of the woman-burden, in pants and short hair. She stood quietly in the ravine while I ran up and down beneath the willow trees. These were the messages she sent me: the cake, the book, the ravine. They reached over that separate residence where she seemed to live, that place where your arms could not reach.

MY mother could not be the mother of three, with the brilliant but drinking and traveling husband, without the sigh, the silence, the inward-turning. The problem was not that she didn't give of herself, but that the role she expected to fill took too much from her. So she cut the sandwich in half, decorated the cake, set out the bowls of paint. You knew a price had been exacted. We didn't know how to feel — lucky to be so gifted, or heavy with debts we couldn't repay?

I felt the most guilty about the obvious childish lusts, like wanting cotton candy in the state fair midway, or fancy patent-leather shoes, or greasy hamburgers from Steak 'n' Shake. I learned to censor my feelings. Forget the ring on the merry-go-round. You could do without it, it's stupid, I'd think to myself. Then I realized that it was not just treats or celebrations that brought out the censor within. It was just about everything. Asking for a sandwich, asking for another blanket on a cold night, asking for the presence of one of my parents.

My mother wouldn't have wished this feeling on me. She would have been ashamed herself, if she knew it was happening. She so wanted to do the right thing. But she was starting at a disadvantage, simply by being a shy person. She could have extended her arms, but part of her was always held back. She was very conscientious, and probably tried to will herself at whatever cost into her ideal of the perfect mother with no desires of her own. The one who took herself to be responsible, single-handedly, for the unfolding psyche of each of her children, and their pressed collars. She was not supposed to be unhappy. This would mean she was a bad mother. So instead, she became hard to locate. She became *far away, across the river.*

YET there were moments when everything seemed in balance. It might have been a day when my brother and sister were older, off to school, my father at work. I had my mother all to myself, and it was very peaceful, eating lunch with her at the yellow breakfast bar, overlooking the field beyond. Sometimes she made me an eccentric lunch. Corncakes with maple syrup. Cream cheese balls, covered in red sugar, mounted on toothpicks, served in a glass dish. We would eat together like conspirators.

The other day, I gave my own young son that kind of lunch. He and I were alone. We put the plates down on the wood table. I made him a sandwich in the shape of two little triangles. "Oh," he said, "a triangle sandwich," his face lit entirely with delight. I kissed his forehead, and I knew that kiss had its source in Beryl Charlotte, the one who sometimes made pancakes in the shape of a rabbit, and the feeling of eminence I had, at that lunch, on a sunlit day in 1955, and other moments when I did receive a gift as freely given as the sun that shone through clear glass, on white tiles, in the stillness of noon.

THE day at home progressed. I went out in the yard, dug up some worms, made caves inside bushes. Maybe a friend from down the street came over and we played cowboys and Indians. Painted a picture. Wandered around in circles, getting a little bored. Watched my mother do one of the more interesting household chores, like pound meat, or pinch leaves off strawberries.

After lunch the minutes seemed to stretch out, because it led up to the daily visit to my father's mother, who was in a nursing home nearby. She was now in her eighties, and sat in a chair. She seemed to remember nothing and no one, said nothing but a low, constant, murmurous moan, and reached for my hands sometimes, as if she were gradually slipping. We always arrived at two o'clock, when the organ fanfare for *The Secret Storm* was cranking up on the TV set there. The place smelled sour and old. There were many people there who mistook you for one of their own relatives, called out, put their arms out. It was my father's mother, but my mother and I visited. It was not clear that it mattered to my grandmother one way or another if we were there. I had heard from my sister and brother that she had once been different. She lived in our house for a while, rocking in the sunlight, keeping them company, and even crocheting a tiny green-and-black rug for my sister's dollhouse. But now, it was not clear to me where she was, what she had ever been.

I never heard her speak clearly. Just some low moaning, and a little grasping, with long, thin hands, hilled with blue veins. The same hands that had pounded meat for my father, or combed her daughter's wavy hair.

This was the low point of the day, and my dread of it is the only reason I can think of for my mother letting me watch, beforehand, a lot of TV programs that weren't really intended for children, like *The Ann Sothern Show*, *Mr. and Mrs. Charles*, and *The Millionaire*. I was seduced by the black-and-white pictures of adult life they offered, people dressed in sharky suits with shoulder pads, hats at an angle, opening and closing the doors of taxicabs, on their way to a doorway in a sunlit city street, everyone with a mission. Nothing like the formlessness of my own household, where my mother was vaguely off in the kitchen doing something. Then it was time to leave for the nursing home.

On the way home from visiting my grandmother, we might stop off at the corner grocery store. This was a tiny place with a butcher counter and sawdust on the floor, where my mother bought me a box of animal crackers and seemed to have long and boring discussions about that most boring subject, meat. My father was fussy about it, bordering on dictatorial. Not too tough. Enough fat. The right kind of cut for sauerbraten. The appropriate grain for a pork chop. Oxtail for soup. Meat had always figured prominently in his Depression stories: "We were poor, but my mother managed to save me a pork chop." The butcher's name was Henry, and I remember my mother saying, "Oh, Henry, we were so disappointed in last week's chops," and Henry looked so downcast, then so determined to improve, that it seemed certain that the next parcel of meat, wrapped in heavy paper and tied with a string, would restore my family to perfect balance.

THIS daily routine was sometimes moderately entertaining, sometimes very boring. But the day was broken up by highlights. A cardinal in the pine tree outside. Hailstones, beating on the bay window, as I sat next to my mother on the piano bench while she played "Molly Malone." Six crystal arms of a snowflake, caught on a scrap of black velvet. But more hours ticked away, with a desolate feeling of walking around in circles on the floor, of reaching into drawers for clues, searching for something that was missing. Two people in a house who were not really together. I might be upstairs, sitting on a very clean and shiny wooden floor, dressing up dolls. She'd be downstairs, paying the household bills with her accordion file out on the dining-room table. I'd be out back, digging swimming holes, or making a village out of old dog bones. She would be inside cooking dinner. I'd be on the porch painting a picture, and she'd be in the kitchen phoning her mother.

I don't think that she tried to think of ways to avoid me. I think that this was her concept of being a good mother, that you raised your child to be "good," and not too demanding of you, not too hungry for your attention. It was one of the hallmarks of efficiency as a mother: clean house, home-cooked food, unobtrusive child. I was not all tangled up with her, hands stuck with flour and batter, or helping her clean her shoes, or both of us with our faces full of fur, discussing the cat's tail. Maybe proximity just bothered her. After all, her own mother was the one able to limit her phone conversations with her distraught, lost, and widowed daughter to exactly three minutes.

THOUGH my father was the official family traveler, my mother clearly accepted the value of transport. Maybe she really was like my father. Perhaps she would have felt happiest when train wheels were turning underneath her. But her job was to be the stationary object, the one who filled glass dishes with rhubarb, in preparation for my father's comings and goings. And for her children's comings and goings, as they ran from door to door, from the doors of the house to the field and streets beyond.

At home, she became a secretly traveling mother, placing herself, despite being in the same room, someplace else. If we were together in the kitchen, she would be stationed by the window over the sink, ready to leave. In the dining room, which had one window that looked out back, her ear was trained on the field behind. Upstairs, in her bedroom with the rose-patterned wallpaper, she seemed to wait for the book she planned to write to arrive. The piano let her travel with the most speed and distance, to the city in music called "The Gates of Kiev," or to that point in the song "Cockles and mussels, alive, alive O." Or to that mysterious place "Song Without Words," where the music would go on and on, the song on and on, with no explanation.

And so my mother taught us to travel as well. There were books and music to carry you away. There was the field beyond the house, where she let us run at will. There were trips to the corner, trips to the city, weekly trips to see my grandmother. We children each had an idea of ourselves we could travel to, away from the centrifugal point of our house: my sister, an interpreter at the United Nations, my brother, with the U.S. Weather Service, myself, a writer of stories in New York. And we took the literal trips, the family vacations, that we all agreed were the best part of the year. In the full force of travel, my parents were zestful and imaginative. To Colorado for mountains and horses. To South Dakota for Mount Rushmore and buffaloes. To Michigan for the lake and blueberries. To the Shenandoah Mountains for their blue mist.

Part of my mother's job on a trip was to make sure the children did not "ruin" the escape plan. My father had fixed goals, even on trips. He liked to get in about four to five hundred miles of driving a day. He was apt to get insensible if his goal was not met, especially if it was his own fault. One night things were not going well. He had miscalculated. His five hundred miles were supposed to be over by nightfall, but they weren't. We had already had dinner, he had already had a few beers. No motels in sight, but we had to keep going. There was nothing but darkness and some flat land outside. My mother had shifted to the backseat, to keep me company. She and the older children played a word game called Ghost, which itself seemed ghostlike to me, since I didn't really understand how it was played yet, as if something thin and white might emerge from the dark flat land outside, as a message.

But now things were changing outside. Heavy rain out of nowhere, in gales that covered the windows of the car. It was getting cold. Other cars were pulling over to let the rain pass. We thought that stopping seemed like a good idea, but my father said we had to keep going. Cold air and silence fell between all of us, and we were all on our own in the moving machine. We knew we had to keep quiet, or my father would just get touchy, a bad situation on a dark night in a car when you can't see in front of you. My legs were bare from wearing shorts. I told my mother I was cold. There were a few old newspapers on the floor of the car. She picked them up and arranged them over my legs. This made them only a little warmer, and much time seemed to go by.

"You're a good traveler," my mother said. I had not complained. It was a rare thing, a direct compliment from my mother. Now the storm was clearing up, and we began to feel that our father would find his way again. I understood it to mean that being a good traveler, a good member of my family, meant learning to travel away from that moment, that very moment, where you did not want to be. It might mean learning to live without my family. In the years to come, I would become an even better traveler, traveling far

enough away from them, to my future perfect place. I often forgot
them entirely, and those moments. Traveling was never difficult.
The problem was arriving someplace, and having to stay.

MY mother's image as the stay-at-home mother was so carefully
constructed that it seemed to imply lost currents, maybe the traveling currents, underneath. Hat and gloves required to go shopping
for a lampshade at Stix, Bauer, and Fuller, or even for liverwurst at
Kroger's. For the home, a pressed blouse, straight skirt, stockings,
and pumps. She did not let loose in pedal pushers, Bermuda shorts,
or ballooning skirts — she was in her forties in the 1950s, and designed
herself as a respectable, classic matron. Red lipstick, powder to
combat a shiny nose, but never a touch of eye makeup. She thought
it too brassy, as she did dangling earrings. She looked irreproachable, her house was very clean, and she was doing her utmost to help
her children. She clipped out articles from the *Post-Dispatch* by noted
child psychologists. She provided flute lessons for the older daughter, math tutoring for the son, nursery school for the younger daughter,
Ethical Culture Sunday school for the whole family. On Sunday,
dinner around a big table with her mother. She didn't gossip with
the neighbors, had no card games with friends and hardly any nights
out with my father. She did not go back to school.

The harder it became to do things, to fix the bacon, decide on a
suit, reason with an angry teenage daughter who wanted to tease
her hair up even higher, chase the cat out of the garage, persuade
her son to do his homework, wait for her husband to get back from
Cuba, set the spoons next to the knives for the millionth time, time
an egg for exactly three and a half minutes, think of something to
have for dinner, write a letter to her sister in Iowa full of cheerful
family news, roll those socks for her husband's next trip to Milwau-

kee — the harder it got, the easier it got, because she would be less and less hounded by desire. She had wanted to write. She had trained to have a job. She wanted to go back to college. The harder it got, the more grateful she would have been just to get through. To finish that mending. Conclude another meal. Put on her hat and gloves. Find the right pair of saddle shoes for her daughter to wear to school. The more despairing, the more grateful. To be able to take a nap every afternoon on the couch, to go to bed early at night. How could you work, anyway, if you needed a nap in the afternoon? To draw the walls of that little house around her, as if they were arms. To be grateful she didn't have to go out there, to earn a living, in that way that only knowledgeable men with slide rules like my father were able to do.

Maybe she had started out just like my father, maybe they were soulmates who should have been bums riding around on freight cars together, the wheels of trains always underneath, instead of standing up as the world's most conscientious, ethical, progressive parents. Instead of building a house, so very, very hard, at such cost, each brick traded for years of transport, years of the turning wheels. My father's wanderlust worked its way into his stories, his nights in strange bars in strange cities. My mother's went right underneath the Saks Fifth Avenue suit, right under the rose bush planted outside the kitchen, right under the geranium by the front door. It came out every now and then, with her children, in those little moments of transport, when she read to us at night, picked a song at the piano, or pointed out a leaf or snowflake.

Once she brought out a book from her childhood called *The Blue Bird*. A frightening-looking volume, a frieze of strange characters on the cover, frozen in poses that represented their names. One was called Bread, who looked like a taciturn baker, and sliced bread off his belly. One was named Candy, who had candy canes for fingers that he broke off for children. *The children were on a journey, to a more childlike place than their own childhood.* They were poor. They couldn't afford a Christmas tree. They looked in through a window of a fancy house at someone else's Christmas tree. So they journeyed to this other land, and ate the slices of belly from Bread, and the broken-off fingers from Candy.

My parents were not yet grown enough to be parents, and I believe they were slicing their own bellies and breaking off their fingers to raise us. And not telling each other, not telling anyone, because you really couldn't, because this conversation did not exist, because they were supposed to be lucky and happy after the Depression and the war, in their solid house with their three children.

FOR years I rested all my impressions of my childhood on the memories of excursions. Running in a field of weeds behind our house, snagging my sleeve on blackberry bushes. The park my mother called "the ravine," which had a steep up-and-down hill and willow trees that made hollows. An old cherry tree cast its fruits on the ground there, and she let me run. The names of streets and avenues seemed to open wide with trees, reaching out to foreign cities. Even the local names of St. Louis byways seemed like destiny itself: Lindell Boulevard, Kingshighway, endless journeys, Creve Coeur, deep heart. Or the park with a pond, where the dragonflies and skatebugs moved so slowly on top of the water that they could have belonged to China, or Louisiana. Even the local trips to the corner took us away, to the bakery with a loaf of bread chugging away in the slicing machine, benign coconut cakes and ladies who truly understood the necessity of having one: "What else, dear?" Or the shoe repair, with dank smells of polish, stitching machines, a special occupation with coded words like *cobbler* and *last*.

It was during these times, in the ravine, at the pond, in the field, in the bakery, in a shoe repair, that my mother was most free from that constant noise that must have been inside her head. The noisy river that had risen to the riverbank let up its sound for a little while, at least. And in me, as well.

The Recipe Book

I ONCE made a point of finding a special document in the Emily Dickinson archive at the Frost Library in Amherst. It was a note written by her brother. On the front, in his heavy handwriting, were some notes about what he wanted to have for dinner. They went something like this: mutton is too greasy, roast beef is okay. On the back of this same paper, in hesitant, spiderlike pencil strokes, was a poem written by his sister about a flower called a fringed gentian. Her poem was almost hidden and clearly took second place. This was the poet who wrote things like "They shut me up in prose," and "My brain is giggling — still."

I also spent time looking for out-of-print writings by women radicals of the 1930s. These were women who stood in picket lines in Detroit and New York, trenches in Spain, who complained about the world, and women's position in it, who pointed out that capitalism would flounder without the free labor of demoralized housewives. Who photographed the free day nurseries in the Soviet Union with children forthrightly constructing bridges with their blocks. Who rode mules in Cuba, and who traveled with Chinese peasants during the revolution. They were underground heroes to me, these women who complained out loud and wrote and traveled all over and saw the world firsthand, and understood economics and politics. When I was feeling low and anonymous, it made me feel a little better to spend time with these writers. They were proof that other

women who had been deeply outraged had a thorough and historical explanation for that outrage, a named quantity, as they explained
in pieces like "Women: The Pivot of Capitalism" and "No More
Helling for Me: An Anonymous Letter." They were also ecstatic in
their discoveries — *I Went to the Soviet Arctic!*

I could see that I might still have to yell in obscure places unrecorded, like them. Here was another hard but clear example of
women calling back to an unrecorded, penciled-in place in the books,
or the grocery list. It meant to me that I could be as mad as I
wanted, because somebody else already had been. If I did not suc-
ceed in carving a permanent place for myself in history, I could
know that those women who traveled around the world and wrote
about it fared no better. While these women were traipsing through
Cuba, China, Spain, and the USSR, my mother was dutifully fin-
ishing college, typing in a newspaper office, and setting up housekeeping. The book she "wanted to write" did not get written. I
eventually came to feel that she was outraged as well, but without
words for that outrage, without an explanation.

In fact, it was her daily job to turn her feelings down low, to the
temperature that makes a good stew. She was busy being a linchpin
of capitalism, busy rolling my father's socks and making Jell-O with
canned fruit floating in it, and trying to convince herself that a Phi
Beta Kappa was actually happy filling up all the hours of her day
doing these things. And that she was lucky, had a "nice" home, a
"nice" life, since she didn't have to work. She did not put her
outrage into almost two thousand poems like Emily Dickinson, or
articles for Communist newspapers, or in documenting foreign rev-
olutions, or yelling at strikes — but I believe that her discontent was
swift-moving enough to bring her to any of these points. As it really
was, however, she simply hissed something to me now and then
about waiting to wear patent-leather shoes, or refused to read me
stories about decorous mermaids who had their tongues cut out —

subtle, indirect protest, but not lost on her daughter. Knowing that she lived with a constant urge to write, knowing that she died young at age fifty unrecorded, followed me everywhere, even before she died.

When I went to elementary school, our teacher read us "Mrs. Goose" stories. These were odd tales of a bumbling, dizzy Mrs. Goose. In a typical story, Mrs. Goose would put on her ruffled apron and plan to bring her friend Mrs. Owl a plate of freshly baked oatmeal cookies. But she ate them all as she was walking through the woods to Mrs. Owl's tree. Once she got there, she'd be surprised at her mistake. She didn't even know what she was doing. All she had to say about it was "Oh dear." It was similar to the segment of *I Love Lucy* in which Lucy and Ethel get a job in a candy factory. Someone speeds up the line, and Lucy and Ethel try to eat up the extra candy as it flies by. It was the same message: women don't make it to the end of the mission. They get mixed up along the way.

Right before my mother died, my father said that she spoke about those stories she had wanted to write, but hadn't been able to. Pure regret that couldn't be answered. He tried to answer it and said, "But you have the children." She said, as he told it, "That's not enough." It may have been the strongest, most articulate statement of outrage she had ever made. My father repeated it to me. Maybe this was not the right thing to do, since I was one of the children that weren't "enough." But I think I instantly forgave her. I was a girl, eleven then, and I saw clearly enough what girls couldn't do because they were girls, and what mothers couldn't do because they were mothers. Now she didn't even have a chance. It was disappointing. It seemed so accidental. She had had fifty years to write those stories. She had gotten cancer five years before. When was the time supposed to come? It was as if she were Mrs. Goose, wandering dizzily through the woods of her life, all those years on her mission, not realizing she was eating up all those words, not saving them for someone else along the way, the words that might have helped her, her friends, her children. They were all gone by the time she got there, and what she had to say was "Oh dear," or "That's not enough."

IN the second grade at Thomas Jefferson Elementary School, I had a ferocious crush on my teacher, Mrs. Boycourt, a linear woman in a suede jacket. She was kindly and energetic, and one day decided to show one of my stories to a visiting school superintendent. I had called it "Mrs. Goose Goes to the United Nations." Looking back, it seems to me that even before my mother died, I was trying to make her story have a happier ending. I must have known then that her mission wouldn't be fulfilled. I transformed Mrs. Goose into a different sort of woman from the forgetful one in an apron, eating her plate of cookies on her way to Mrs. Owl's house. My Mrs. Goose was wearing a green turtleneck sweater, to prepare her for difficulties. Despite interventions from foxes and other obstacles, she did make it to the United Nations, where she was given a position that required her to make decisions.

SINCE my mother did not leave behind a book, I try to think of the other books that she did make. The book of her house, the book of her children, the book of her dreams. A little blue box, full of index cards with her handwriting on them. Recipe box, recipe book. I decided to read her recipe book, in order to look for my mother, sister, aunt, grandmother, to dwell with them for a while in the presence of cornmeal weighed in the hand, cherries pitted by the sink. I know full well that I am dealing with only a partial document. Not the whole book, not the whole mother. The reasoned guess and inference, the likely analogies I might make, are only partial gestures in a full portrait. She was someone else entirely that she recognized. To me, she represented earth, the *away, across the river* place, the moon, tall grass growing in the fields, the likelihood of snow or rain. At the same time, she brought forth another day in a house full of nearly burned toast, the same humming refrigerator, the same sunbeam through the window shortly after noontime, the same rooms that, though small, and tightly furnished, made the sound of your feet hollow when you walked through, that did not yield the secrets and information that you really needed.

The pouring of milk for children, the bleaching of their shoe-laces, and the wiping of linoleum countertops did not yield the secrets and information my mother needed. Yet, this was all she was supposed to do. The conflict seemed to dampen her so much that gradually she came to feel that this was all she could do. And certainly, if she looked at a women's magazine of the era, or read a new recipe book, or one handed down from her own family, it was implied that this was all she should do. Even the plain, seasonless, hygienic menus of the fifties seemed to imply that this was enough: food without flavor, white bread like a sponge, shapes without content, weight on the plate without desire to eat it.

IN Betty Crocker's "Bisquick Party Book," dated 1957, a mother's cooking was a test. So much depended upon turning the petals of a tuna tulip. Recipes are prefaced with breathless introductions: "Spicy hamburger filling bakes under the crust ... but ends up on top." This description implies an easy-to-surprise, small-town naiveté on the part of the housewife, thrilled to find that the hamburger made its way to the surface. Bringing food to the table was a way of checking to see if this woman was the right kind of woman: "Canned chicken and frozen vegetables for the easy party dish that makes a calm hostess." A sigh of relief, opening the can, cracking the paper on the frozen vegetable box. The housewife's job went hand in hand with ideas of progress that gave people new ways not to speak to each other: "Parties . . . [are] much more fun nowadays with the trend toward informal entertaining. Good food and good companionship are shared before a television set. . . ."

Food was not just food. It represented the lack of worldliness in the right kind of woman, someone able to be surprised when the hamburger floated to the top of the pie, or the pineapples turned up on the top of the upside-down cake. Proper food showed that the housewife could do her job, to serve germ-free food without too much excitement to her family and friends, to be the "calm hostess." It represented the right thing to do.

My mother was not without knowledge of the world. Yet she left the city for the suburbs, she left what she learned to try to be gratified when the cake rose, the popovers popped. Was it enough? I don't think so. Yet she persisted in the idea, year after year, that it would be. Except for the sighs, and the unwritten book, and the regret when she didn't go back to school. My parents liked to view themselves as discerning, even immune from popular trends. But maybe the idea of the sheltered, doelike homemaker was something they couldn't help but try to live out, after the war, and after the Depression.

Certainly, there were other contradictions. They viewed Eisenhower as a warmonger, and campaigned for Adlai Stevenson. Yet they let me watch all the paranoia-inducing invader-from-outer-space movies I wanted. They never took me to see animated Disney movies, saying that they ruined your imagination. But they did purchase a stand-up TV tray, and let me eat on top of it, even watching Walt Disney at Sunday dinnertime, alone. At the time I thought this was a big treat, but I now recall it as a strange and lonely experience, eating chicken and mashed potatoes with Hayley

Mills, or Spin and Marty, while the rest of the family ate together in the dining room.

EXPLORING the metaphor of the meal begins to explain the enshrinement of my mother's recipe box in our house. Looking through it now, I find a similar vein of tension, as in Betty Crocker's advice — do this the right way, or else: DO NOT OVERBEAT, or <u>Sift before measuring,</u> underlined with red grease pencil. Or, a warning concerning pineapple upside-down cake, from my mother's mother: "By putting whole pineapple rings together, you minimize danger of their moving and becoming disarranged." This exacting mother, who sewed hems with stitches as evenly spaced as the teeth of a comb, left her echoes in the recipes: "Mother says use double boiler and let it boil five minutes on the *top* of the double boiler." Maybe my mother felt as if she had her mother looking over her shoulder every minute, ready to scold her.

My mother also dutifully applied her college skills to the job of cooking. She clipped an article from the newspaper that begins "There is no way of preparing meat more appealing than really delicious pot roast" and she underlined the really crucial parts, about adding onions at the last ten minutes of browning, and adding enough liquid for the "incomparable 'roast' flavor." She drew diagrams of Christmas cookies, like biology drawings, except instead of a straight line leading to the heart or aorta, there is a line drawn indicating where the blue sugar tips of a star should go, or how little holly leaves should spring from a red-hot. She made notes on special procedures: "For Christmas boxes, Edna S. decorates with Curtiss Michigan Cherries, 10 cents a bag at Sewing's drugstore." In the corners of the recipe cards, she noted results: "good." "<u>Good.</u>" "Excellent."

There was precision to her filing system, maybe borne from

secretarial experience, or from a sense of the seriousness of this job: "Lettuce, Wilted, Mother's," filed under L in the vegetable section. Her calculations of serving sizes showed an odd attention to detail. One recipe was said to "serve three and a half" — who was the half person? For backup, when memory failed, my mother kept separate cards with lists of the everyday sandwiches — salami, ham, egg and tomato, cheese, roast beef. Or different combinations of fruit cups — oranges, pears, apples — and weekday desserts — canned peaches, Jell-O, tapioca pudding. This business of meals was not something that seemed to come naturally to her. She seemed to be preparing herself for an exam: "What are ten desserts that may be served Monday through Friday?" "What are your husband's favorite sandwiches?" She had even filled in a list to answer this last question, in order of preference. Sometimes she calmed her worries with a clipping from the newspaper: "Roasting a Turkey Isn't the Easiest Job in the World."

The pressures revealed in the Betty Crocker pamphlet were public — dealing with the test of womanhood (a real woman is not too worldly, and she worries about pleasing other people). But the additional messages I find in my mother's recipe box had more to do with being a good woman in the eyes of her family, and, more specifically, in the eyes of her very demanding mother. Food was the way to remain connected to dead and distant relatives, to prove your familial allegiances. The good daughter-in-law took down the recipe for "Mother N.'s Sauerbraten." The good daughter copied the instructions for marble cake, the special, hard-to-bake cake served only, ceremoniously, for someone's birthday. The favored niece of an aunt in California preserved the recipe for "Aunt Charlotte's Stewed Chicken and Dumplings." The good wife clipped recipes for something a little more exotic to impress the boss, like "Company Pork Chops," distinguished by canned cream of mushroom soup. The harried housewife clipped recipes from the sides of boxes, for things made out of cans of soup and Minute rice. The good mother made baked custard for children with sore throats. The good daughter-in-law, daughter, wife, mother, efficient housewife cooked every day.

But where was Beryl Charlotte herself? Was any of this food made for her? I do not recall her ever lifting the lid of a pot to sniff fragrant steam and say "Delicious." I do not recall her being thrilled when the cake rose, or enjoying making pink roses out of icing on a birthday cake. I do not recall her ever lighting into anything she cooked with speed, hunger, or obvious satisfaction. I do recall frozen peas rolling across my plate, uneaten, dried-out pork chops, hunks of mashed potatoes, bizarre salads with Jell-O in them served on top of an iceberg lettuce leaf. It was more from a sense of duty than hunger, or certainly not pleasure, that I ate these things, and perhaps it was only a dull sense of duty, bordering on resentment, that impelled my mother to cook them. There was not enough information or mystery for her, coming from Betty Crocker, or from the recipe for a tuna noodle casserole.

THE cuisine represented in my mother's box falls into roughly three categories: old family recipes, recipes thought to be fancy and reserved for yearly business dinners when the boss came, and recipes that incorporated technological food feats of the 1950s. There were curious amalgams of the unusual and the mundane: "Veal Cutlets with Catsup," "Scalloped Cabbage with Bacon Chips," "Veal Loaf," "Mexican String Beans." And clever recipes for fake pies, fake cakes: "mock apple pie, " made from twenty Ritz crackers, "crushed fine." Or refrigerator "cakes," which were really store-bought chocolate cookies layered with whipped cream that expanded overnight in the refrigerator into a "cake." The directions for these recipes are often surprisingly painstaking, filled with precision and emphatic direction. The recipe for peanut butter cookies, clipped from a magazine, adds this note on quantity: "Yield — 67 cookies." And on design: "Press in two directions with fork." Not one direction, or none at all. My mother kept a running conversation with herself about success and failure. For "Ranger Cookies," she says, "Try hotter oven? Mine took too long to bake at 350." She did not gossip with neighbors, hang on the phone or over the fence, lunch with colleagues, or play cards routinely. She saw her old college friends once or twice a year. Through the fabric of food, she kept a conversation going with herself.

There were ethical concerns as well. Betty Crocker, though occasionally called upon, was regarded as not the real thing, a cheaper, cut-rate version of real food. Newspaper recipes were avoided, since my mother had worked at a newspaper and knew that whole recipes were sometimes ruined by a typographical error. Real food came from the recipe box, from the kitchen of Grandma, or Aunt Charlotte, or Edna S., or Ida K. Real birthday cakes did not come from the bakery or a box. They were usually marble or angel food cakes, made with much lengthy mixing and beating. Separate bowls, flour sifters, the mysterious moment of "folding" the fluffy eggwhites, and a certain amount of anxiety about the outcome. An angel food cake with seventeen hand-beaten egg whites that flopped in the oven was one day's worth of disaster. Once, my grandmother baked her usual marble cake, which called for two different batters "put into tube pan in alternate spoonfuls." But this time it failed to bake up with the desired handsome black-and-white marble effect. Instead, it was a uniform sandy brown color. Same taste, but no marbles. This clearly ruined my grandmother's day. "I was so disappointed," she said, over and over throughout the afternoon. "So much work." When the birthday cakes worked, as they usually did, they were the pure, clear embodiment of maternal love, much more festive than having your ears cleaned or the mud scraped from your shoes.

The "Mother N." recipes were from my father's side of the family. They documented his history on the farm in Illinois, or in a Depression household — doughnuts fried in a pound of lard, cheap cuts of meat transformed, as in "Spareribs with Sauerkraut" or "Mock Swiss Steak." I had heard, once, of his being taken as a boy to visit friends of his parents, who were very poor, and who offered them a pound cake made with bacon grease. "A terrible smell," he said, and it was understood that nothing like that would happen in our hygienic, middle-class home of the fifties, as we unwrapped sticks of pure yellow butter for the statuesque marble cake, and did not have to pull pinfeathers out of old chickens.

WRITING down recipes on a recipe card was very exhilarating to me as a child. I could be part of what was handed down, the mysterious order of women held together with crochet hooks, flour sacks, and rug yarn. Recipe cards, not baseball cards, not dollar bills, not stocks and bonds, were what women traded among themselves. If you could write one out, you could join your aunts, grandmothers, mothers, sisters. My mother and my aunt applied themselves studiously to this exchange.

My mother sometimes folded a letter from her sister in between the index cards in her box. One included recipes, and a discussion on the merits of chili powder versus paprika to give scalloped potatoes the right color. It also mentioned that out-of-town friends were visiting, but as her husband could not come, she would not go out to dinner with them. How were these two women, one trained in college as a chemist, one trained in college as a teacher and for a time employed by a major city newspaper, brought together to write each other on this ground? Once they were sisters who had dug in the mud together on the shore of a lake in Missouri. They had sat together in the second-floor window seat on Hebert Street and looked out as the streetcar muffled by in the snow. Inside the cover of the fairy-tale book with the mermaid on the cover, they had both left their autographs written above and below the clouds printed upon the page. They had both been stopped short by the words of a mother who sewed hems onto crepe de chine with nearly invisible stitches. Now they were grown women, the women of the house, maybe trying on these preoccupations with scalloped potatoes in the same way that small girls put on their mother's high heels. They convinced each other that they were mature, "capable" women who now traded new secrets. They told each other that these were the words that now held them together.

MY sister surprised us all and dropped out of college suddenly to be a wife and a mother. The same girl who said she'd like to be an interpreter at the United Nations turned into a woman overnight at age nineteen, pregnant, suddenly obsessed with cooking, Catholicism, ironing a man's shirts, and the tiny garments of infants. She couldn't have thought of a better affront to my mother. She arrived with a beehive hairdo, Cleopatra liner around the eyes, and a madras maternity shift she had made herself from her dormitory bedspread. My mother thought girls should go to college first. Certainly be married before pregnant, and not make their maternity clothes out of old bedspreads.

My sister swerved into her new domestic role with a vengeance. She even sent my mother recipes for dishes she thought to be a little more exotic, modern, and flamboyant than my mother's stalwart meat-potatoes-and-cake routine. File cards arrived in the mail with instructions for cream puffs, or chili con carne, written with enthralled comments: "Dump in flour, beat batter like mad." Or, typed up on the red ribbon of the typewriter, and showing her up as an excellent, worldly, if barefoot kind of housewife: "Buy Rinaldo's tomato sauce, available in St. Louis." My mother was without a doubt heartbroken that her oldest bright girl had left college — that place always mentioned in our house with reverence — the place that saved girls from trailer parks — and married a promising but broke student. That her daughter had been dreaming up long, complicated names for her baby, Angelina Rose, Maria Angelina, instead of conjugating French verbs. That she had immersed herself in comparing the relative virtues of brands of canned tomatoes instead of Shakespeare's plays. That she had spent time converting to the mysteries of Roman Catholicism instead of pondering Ethical Culture. Despite all these reservations, my mother accepted the recipes as a currency of exchange from her wayward daughter. She didn't throw them out or ignore them. She tried them out, dutifully recording the results the way she always did: "Good — 50 minutes too long — cook with lid of pot cracked so doesn't dry out." Maybe even wrote back to my sister, something polite like "Thank you for the chili recipe, it was very good."

A sister well versed in chemistry, a rebellious daughter with a new baby on her hip, ancient relatives with names like Ida, a little daughter who wanted to be in the rodeo — all could meet in my mother's recipe box, in peace, under the guise of being good women. And there are moments when we still meet in the scent of frying onions, the color of new blackberries picked for jam, the sound of an egg beaten in an earthenware bowl, the ascent of flour dust toward the noonday sun.

THE recipe box was a book that many women wrote, and that few ever really read. In between its pages, I find glimpses of a woman, alone in her kitchen, at a stray time, say eleven-fifteen in the morning or four-thirty in the afternoon, alone or surrounded by children circling her feet, or crying, or asking her to read a book, tie a shoe, button doll clothes, or answer a question like "Do children ever die?" Or for jelly sandwiches, or to sing songs about men and bones rolling home. Maybe she takes out a page of her book, and turns it into the dinner that the two-year-old ignores, the husband eats without comment, the older children parcel out in secret to the dog. Or maybe the children shovel it down happily like workers, or the boss who comes to dinner compliments her, and her husband beams down at her. So the book goes, the page returned to its place in the file.

But "There was something I wanted to write" was still the refrain that lingered in my house, despite the success of "Company Pork Chops" or "Mrs. Klausman's Parker House Rolls." And it was the refrain of regret, of the undone, of inarticulate desire that seemed to take a little air out of the popovers, that toughened the roast a bit, or made the cheese sauce flat and bland. These scraps of paper may have been everywoman's book, but they did not provide the language of desire for every woman. Consider the distance between these titles, for example: My mother, 1939, "Lettuce, Wilted, Mother's," and Ruth Gruber, 1939, *I Went to the Soviet Arctic!* My mother, 1938, "Mother N's Mock Swiss Steak," and Agnes Smedley, 1940, *China Fights Back.* There was a continent to leap between my mother's kitchen and these other women's lives. She didn't make the leap. Nor did she find a way to negotiate a middle distance, some way to write in between the meat loaf and the indefinite arc of her aspirations. Emily Dickinson just turned her brother's list of favorite dinners over and wrote a poem on the back. I didn't find any of these in my mother's file. She had vague ideas for books, "children's stories," she would say. Sometimes she read one of my children's library books with a professional, appraising eye. Once I found a little slip of paper from a memo pad. It seemed that she had started what was meant to be a collection of stories of the holidays for children. This one was the story of Saint Valentine.

I think it is really true that I once spent a Valentine's Day with her inside a warm brick house on a snowy day, that we really baked heart-shaped cookies and iced them with pink icing, and that I really held one in my hand as I looked out the window at the snow coming to rest on the tangly branches of a Japanese quince bush. About seven or eight years after that Valentine's Day, I would make a Valentine for her in school, a red paper heart pasted on a white lace doily, with a message written in white ink, some little message from a child who did best in writing. I thought she needed it. She was sick, and I was not prone to lavish demonstrations of affection. But a red paper heart was okay. She died a few days before Valentine's Day, the day of the story of the saint that she had once tried to record, on a little slip of paper. The red paper curled up by the windowsill, with no place to go. We were all convinced that these pieces of paper, red hearts, file cards in a box, memo pads with unfinished stories, or the ones that never got filled with words, could make such a difference.

THE recipe box wasn't a big enough book for my mother. It wasn't big enough for my sister, despite her fervent attempts to out-mom my mother at the age of nineteen, with perky notes on cream puffs and spaghetti sauce. She went after domestic life in a big way, but it didn't work. Eventually she would ransack each nest she made, blow down every roof over her head. My aunt rebelled, too, more quietly. For many, many years after her husband's sudden death, she lived in her own house as if she were only a temporary visitor.

My grandmother had drawn designs for elaborate dresses. My mother wanted to write. My aunt was a promising chemist. My sister wanted to be an interpreter at the UN. I wanted to be a doctor. But what we were really supposed to do was cook. My father tried to be progressive about me, the upstart daughter who wanted to be a doctor. "You can do anything you want," he'd say, but what made him really happy, when the tone and tenor of his voice would change, was the moment his small girl made him a sandwich for lunch. All of us, dress designer, writer, chemist, interpreter, doctor, were taught how to title a recipe card, to list ingredients, to hope for a favorable outcome, as if the success or failure of the height of the popover, the marbles in the marble cake, the markings that said A on an apple pie, marked the degree of recompense for all that was left undone.

Ida Lupino

I INHERITED a red Schwinn with fat tires from my older sister. It had a world-worn look to it by the time I got it, with many dents on the fenders. My brother told me these were the results of her recklessness. There were some concrete stairs built into the hill on the side of the schoolyard. About fifteen steps, a landing, and fifteen steps more, and steep. My brother said my sister used to ride her bike down those steps so she could speed out onto the field.

I learned to ride in the schoolyard field. It was a little dizzying at first, but there were always the soft mounds of spring grass to cushion a fall. It was my freedom, a horse, a truck, a train, a freight car. As soon as I kicked off, the streets and trees opened up, and the stationary, solitary little house receded into the landscape, just part of the cardboard backdrop.

My best friend, Margery, lived six houses down the street. I met her at school. Before that, I played only with boys, because they lived directly across the street, and my mother looked no further for my playmates. Cowboys and Indians. Now that I had Margery, we could develop our parallel interests. We played round after round of War, Fish, or Old Maid on the curb. Her father had a canister of poker chips, so we moved on to poker. She owned a special future-predicting ball that was supposed to look like an eight ball for pool. When you rolled it around in your hands, fortune-telling messages would appear in a window in the ball, with vague predictions like "crazy eights," "yes," "no," "you'll see," "try again," and "maybe." We were so devoted to our daily poker games that we couldn't imagine a future without them. One day we spent an afternoon working with the fortune-teller so it would definitely say "yes" when we asked it, will we live next door to each other when we grow up?

Aside from playing cards and predicting our future, we were also in complete accord about what constituted a satisfying bike ride. First we each asked our mothers to give us a dime. We put it in a sock, for later, and it eventually slid into our shoes. Then we met at Margery's driveway, since it was on the way. Now we were riding past our school, which looked shut-faced and strange on a Saturday afternoon, all its secrets locked up in the utility closets. Now we turned left up the hill leading to the busy roads, Lucas and Hunt Boulevard. Houses with their peaked gables and occasional turrets, covered by fat, dense pine trees, looked like castles to us. Now we turned onto a wide road with a broad island of green park in the middle. On the island, there were trees, bushes, intrigue, and sour cherries that hung down to be picked in the summer. Alongside the island were wide sidewalks for the fat tires of our bicycles, a wide road, trees to the left, to the right, and named *Boulevard,* which meant something about Paris. Something about infinity, far away from landlocked Missouri, the squatty-looking middle state on the map.

Now we were getting excited, because we were close to the main drag, home of the post office. The lobby held hundreds of little boxes lined with fancy brass, equipped with secret lock combinations, and visited by mysterious people who did not wait for their mail at home. People with suits and business to attend to, like on *Mr. and Mrs. North* or *The Millionaire.* But the biggest thrill was examining the WANTED posters for woman criminals. Here were true-life bad girls, even worse than Barbara Stanwyck or Ida Lupino, snarling in the movies, first in sequined nightclub gowns, and then in prison garb. Their lives were without a doubt more interesting than my mother's, checking to see if the pot roast had dried out. The dozens of sorting bins and shelves behind the front windows confirmed my idea that our local post office was a major terminus, connected not obscurely at all to streets and boulevards worldwide.

Next came a strip of stores and that most modern of places, Kroger's Supermarket. We had already been there with our mothers and peered at cans of peas and carrots stacked in pyramids. It was a wholesome but faintly ominous place. Some place where Barbara Stanwyck, bad girl, negotiated a murder while wearing cat-style sunglasses, her hair rolled like sausages, in *Double Indemnity.* Kroger's was our first stop for spending the dime, which by now had settled toward the bottom of our shoes. We preferred the older dimes, maybe worn a little thin, but with a profile of what we thought of as a beautiful woman with wings, really winged Mercury. But we took what we could get.

At Kroger's, we each ordered one slice of liverwurst at the cold-cut section, which cost three cents. The butcher patiently wrapped each slice in brown paper and taped it up. We progressed directly to the checkouts, to pick up a Zero candy bar, a white chocolate-covered affair with a picture of a polar bear on the package. Four cents left. Then we moved down the strip to Schmidt's Bakery, where we always went with our mothers to buy boring things like bread and coconut cakes, where we were now at liberty to select any color of cupcake we wanted — pink, peach, yellow, or white — and check out the tired-looking bride-and-groom sets that posed on the shelf for forthcoming wedding cakes. Another three cents and a little white bag to add to our parcels. We sat on the curb and ate everything. Then we stopped in a tiny luncheonette, where our parents would never go because of the alleged grease. We sat on red swivel chairs at the counter, and ordered water, which they always gave us with ice, and left the remaining penny on the counter as a courtesy. We had seen something about leaving money on counters in the movies, maybe *Mildred Pierce* or *The Postman Always Rings Twice,* and knew that eating at a counter required a certain know-how.

The ride home brought us under the shade of the boulevard trees again, drawn into the green arcade away from our delicious taste of the world at large, skin of liverwurst peeled away, brown paper unwrapped, cars avoided in the parking lot, cupcake unwrapped, post office looming with intrigue and the possibility of crime, of being a big-time bad girl, washed down with a greasy water glass at the lunch counter, which might be a train car leading away to anywhere, more poker games, state prison, Hollywood, who could tell? We welcomed the arms of those trees, the innocent branches hanging low with cherries. We returned to our houses. For now, we would help our mothers set the table for dinner, set out food for the cat, and sleep in our beds between smooth ironed sheets, under quilts made by our grandmothers. The next Saturday, we would do all of these things, in the same order, all over again, until we could become the beautiful woman on the dime, or Ida Lupino.

All About Me

THE story about my father that followed us around the house all the time, when we opened the door to the refrigerator, or painted white polish on our saddle shoes, was about his life during the Depression. I saw the house where my father spent those years on Penrose Street only once. In the 1950s, my father still owned it, and kept some elderly lady tenants. We went to fix some plumbing. The ladies were very sweet, and the apartment was the most dreary home I had ever set foot in. The bricks on the outside were now yellow and gray, having weathered sooty St. Louis when it was known as "TB City." Everything looked worn, faded, and thin. Pale brown flowers receding into the wallpaper, thin linoleum on the floor, worn-down thresholds between the rooms, a dim view of the neighbor's brick wall through the window. It was only nine miles, really, but far from our chintz and mint-green rooms in suburbia, from the kitchen window with a view of rabbits in the brush field.

So there it was that he had spent those years — working six and a half days a week, nights filled with a cheap cut of meat, night school, church youth group, at something called Pentecostal, Evangelical, writing a furious, high-toned letter to the editor of the *Post-Dispatch* that might or might not get read. The stories of his earlier days had joy in them — about sitting out on the porch, in Edwardsville, Illinois, in 1919 or so, with his mother and father resting after the day, playing in a thick patch of four-o'clocks, looking for toads.

And happier city days as well — after they moved to St. Louis, spending a Saturday hopping on and off freight cars in the train yards, stopping off at the American Biscuit Company cookie factory and buying a bag of broken cookies for a penny, walking the streets, and eating them. Our father had never eaten with us on a weekday, since he was always off with Mr. Braviano or Mr. Werner at some dark and red businessman's lunch lounge, or the cafeteria of Anheuser-Busch or Pearl Brewing. This story seemed to imply an entirely different kind of life in the old days, with less distance than in the lives of suburban fathers who disappeared into the city to work, when you could just run down the street and eat with your father, sitting practically in the dirt. Sometimes, on Saturdays, my father seemed to try to make up for this, but in a more civilized, suburban way. He wore an old red corduroy shirt, with the radio tuned to the Metropolitan Opera broadcast, and fixed us some kind of sandwich that only fathers liked — sardines, chipped beef, or maybe the famous sausage and jelly — and opened a bottle of beer. He poured it into a glass "correctly," down the side of the glass, with no head.

BUT the Depression stories had no sandwiches eaten together in the noonday sun, no fooling around on freight cars. The story was stuck on the continuous refrain of not being able to finish college, and we picked up that my father viewed night school as second-rate, piecemeal. When he was offered a chance to go away to seminary, it was a way to get the education he longed for, to stay in a universe of books and thoughts. But his mother wouldn't let him go. And it was this setting down of his own deep wish, for his mother's survival, that followed us everywhere. He never finished college, a thought that plagued him nonstop, we thought. The fact that my father made this sacrifice in the Depression seemed to have something to do with opening his beer and settling into it at noontime on a Saturday. Everything was related to the second-rate biology class at night, and staying home when he could have gone away somewhere.

The story rolled out at any given moment, to explain why he was having another beer and staring off into space instead of playing checkers with us. Why he was not pitching baseball on the vacant lot across the street, why we must listen attentively while he narrated the triumphs of his day at work, why he did not ask us about our stories. We had no story to match, because we had not been poor in the Depression. We always had something to look at when we opened the refrigerator door, we always had sturdy, well-made saddle shoes, and a whole other pair for Sunday. Our mother did not nag us every day, and she did not struggle to put meat on the table. So my father fixed his position of being irreproachable. The worse that could happen to any one of us had already happened to him.

When my mother died, when I was eleven, he didn't seem to see a parallel with his own experience. He had lost a father, and the real resulting tragedy was having to become a breadwinner overnight. The strongest indication I had that he understood my loss was that once, in the year after my mother died, I asked if we could have a second cat, which he knew and I knew my mother would not have allowed. He said yes, and I interpreted this to mean that he knew, now that my mother was gone, that I needed something extra. The cat was named Maxine. She was a tricolor cat, which I had read in *The Observer's Book of Cats*, was thought by sailors to be a lucky combination.

EVEN after my mother's death, the Depression story still didn't die. It was the pivot of guilt, the place where we always excused and forgave him, the place where we found our businessman father in a starched white shirt, who signed a brisk "WN" on business memos, to be a fourteen-year-old boy. Skinny, panic-stricken, not knowing what to do, with a mother who fell on top of him as soon as his father died, like an ironing board. We knew he was still looking for someone to tell him he had done the right thing, that he was smart and not lacking. In his later years, his face had a permanently hounded look, as if he were always looking for someone to say well done, okay.

The Depression story rose up every now and then at odd points in daily life. Our tidy suburban house was a mundane fact of existence to us, but to him must have been a concept, an idea of solidity he was trying daily to make concrete. Inside it, little fissures sometimes opened. I was peeling potatoes once, when I was nine. Out of nowhere, my father lit into the bowl of peels, as if he couldn't help himself, held up the skins, and said, "Too thick! Your Grandmother Nekola would never have done it like this. You're taking off too much potato. The skins should be as thin as paper." I wasn't too worried. I knew there were more potatoes under the sink, and that this was the kind of thing that bothered fathers who had been through the Depression. When we wanted to go barefoot in the summer, like Annette Funicello in *Beach Blanket Bingo*, the thought of children who could afford shoes not wearing them irritated him no end. "Put those shoes on!" he'd grouse, and we would resign ourselves to lacing up our brown oxfords again. Anyway, we knew the story had a happy ending.

ACCORDING to the story, the Depression got better and better, thanks to Franklin Delano Roosevelt. My father dabbled in radical politics and "almost" became a card-carrying member of the Communist Party. This astounding fact was always related with great zest, as if the Depression, finally, had been the most exciting time of his life. He worshiped FDR, a "household god," he would say. This was when he rode the train down to see the completion of a Tennessee Valley Authority dam in Norris, Tennessee. He wrote articles about his trip which he hoped would appear in some bastion of quality writing like *The New Yorker*. He recorded his visit to a school that was so sleepy at noontime that "a dog trotted down the hall." In Tennessee, he even fell in love with a woman who had come to see the dam as well, only she had just become a nun. So the story was a mix of pain, and its transcendence, which could certainly never be matched by any of us, sheltered by our little brick house, watching commercials for peanut butter on TV.

It had a happy ending, didn't it? It turned out he had a talent for designing machines, and by the time he was thirty, had several patents and my solid-gold mother to his name. There were awkward moments, when there was a strike at the machinery plant, and he was now management, not a worker. It must have had a happy ending. But why did it keep coming back?

THE story of our father was what we breathed every day more than his presence, since he was gone so often. When he was there, he seemed to be in another stratosphere made up of machine parts and arias from operas, of trains and dusty bakeries and butcher shops, of cities we had never seen, of hops and malt brewing in gigantic vats, of St. Louis in the good moments of his youth, of falling in love with a Russian ballerina, of fixing windowsills in a box-shaped house. He was always hard to locate, even when he was sitting right across the table from you. Somewhere, a long way back, he had developed the habit of not being right there. Of being, instead, in his story.

We children were obliged to continue his story, representing the successful resolution of the Depression. We were proof. Hair parted carefully. Clean, pressed clothes of a good cut. Modern brick house. Collie with shining fur groomed. A mother who didn't work, who would never have to wash another woman's floor, as his mother had done. We would never have to drop out of school. Three tall, happy children who drank pure milk from glass bottles. I bought this story, so much so that I even improved on it. I thought we were just the same as the family in a book on my shelf called *The Small Family*. In the oddly featureless, almost geometric drawings, the Small family looked like streamlined icons. The mother, in a ruffled apron, bringing a steaming bowl of oatmeal to a breakfast table. The husband in a business suit, two children at the table, their clothes as sharp as paper, curtains parting the window above, sunlight streaming onto the cups and saucers. I still sometimes think of my days at home as being exactly like that, cleanly defined, definite, right, satisfying to all members of the Small family, and the Nekola family, the house not really humming with sighs and longward gazes, not really shot through with turning train wheels.

I WENT to school in a plaid dress with a white collar. I loved everything about school and was an exemplary student. In second grade I wrote a story in school, which I later found my father had saved, in a file labeled "Charlotte," among my old report cards, doctor's reports, some pictures I drew, letters I sent him. It seems we had been given the title by our teacher: "All About Me." My account went like this:

"The name 'Nekola' came from Czechoslovakia. The reason there are not many Nekolas in the USA is that the first Nekola to come was my father's grandfather. My father has very, very dark brown hair. He has brown eyes, and he was born in California. His family lived in many places. His sister was shot with a firecracker. So he was an only child. His father died when he was 14. So he went out and got a job. He got his first job at a laundry. But then he broke his wrist and was fired. He thinks that he was fired because they thought that he would sue them. So then he got his job at the Berry Weymiller Machinery Co. He worked there until a strike came. No Beer! So no jobs for the people that worked at Berry Weymiller. They make machines for bottles. Then he got another job until the strike was over. And he's been there ever since."

And so the story of my father had become the bread of life. I wondered how much of my story, even now, was all about me, or all about him. When is it, exactly, that children tell their own story?

RECENTLY, I found that my father had written an "All About Me" story that wasn't really about him, either. My brother and I found a night-school notebook my father had saved since 1933. It was a small green-paper-bound volume, with ruled pages, and notes on subjects like "Primitive Man" and "The Roots of Democracy," taken down in earnest, and biology sketches of cell division. There were poems for English, one called "On Love," another called "To Sandra's Right Hand." And an essay called "My Autobiography." The handwriting was unrecognizable as my father's. The letters looked as if they had been taken from a model alphabet, with none of the improvisations that would come to define his middle-aged scrawl.

Our father had never showed us this essay, but it seemed that he meant for us to find it after he was gone. In his very last years, he took to dating and labeling artifacts of his life that he thought would fall into our hands. So, for example, we found a ceramic dresser box, the kind used for safety pins and paper clips, which was also a model of a pasteurizer my father worked on. He left us a note that said, "Vortex Pasteurizer, WN was responsible for exterior design," describing himself, William Nekola, in the third person. The green notebook was also dated in the handwriting not of the twenty-one-year-old, but of the seventy-year-old, as if he fully expected us to read it someday. We felt miffed: another message from long distance.

Reading this essay was like meeting someone I never knew, my father nineteen years before he was my father. The writing style was stilted, a bit cautious, the work of an anxious twenty-one-year-old who wants to make a permanent impression on his English teacher. His language is humorless, unlike that of the father I knew, who liked sly phrases like "happy as a clam." Reading now, five years since my father's death, having now been, myself, the English teacher who graded autobiographical essays of alienated twenty-one-year-olds for thirteen years, I am not sure how to identify myself. My father's daughter? Colleague of the teacher? Friend of the twenty-one-year-old youth represented therein, who is obviously in trouble? Big sister of lost youth? His teacher wrote, at the top of the page, in red pencil, "Fairly spirited." I rush to defend him — why only "fairly" spirited? Couldn't she have given him more than that?

The more I read, the more I wondered if this story was really the key to his past, more so than any of the other versions of his story, the mound story, or my "All About Me" story. My father said that his days in Collinsville were "the idyllic sort of childhood that authors write about." I am sure that by age twenty-one my father already wanted to be an "author." He had started writing poems and letters to the editor, and here he also rewrote the story of his childhood to match his vision. It is hard to imagine that a man who caused so much trouble to himself, and to those who loved and depended on him, truly had an "idyllic" childhood. But at age twenty-one, this is what I would have said about my early years — the perfect early years when I thought my family was just the same as the Small family, mother and father, sister and brother, eating their oatmeal in the sunny breakfast room.

IN his essay, I think my father meant to project the voice of a young master smoothly in control of his destiny, having lived through the rough parts of his life. He didn't know it, but this voice is not smooth; it cracks, it contradicts itself, it lays bare an open hand. He created himself in later years as the well-heeled businessman, starched white shirt with French cuffs, gold cufflinks, wing-tip shoes, leather briefcase. As the world traveler, he brought us anecdotes about hazelnut soufflé in Vienna, or rum in Cuba. As the cultured businessman, he bought season tickets to the symphony, took his children to see the Lippizaner horses in Washington, repaired a faucet on a Saturday afternoon while listening to the Texaco Star Metropolitan Opera broadcast. Underneath was the thin boy who couldn't lay bricks, always trying to catch up.

My father claimed in his essay that he held an exalted position in his own family as a young child, and was brought up very short when he had to step out into the world — first school, then work. He was "the son who was their whole interest in life," an "only child who had been given a superiority complex by indulgent parents." He speculates on his early, exceptional training: "My parents were both ambitious for my early maturity, so it was not difficult to understand the easel slate that became mine when I was four years old. On it my mother and I spent many busy hours while I delightedly pursued the mysteries of the alphabet...."

This is the story my father built, the house my father built, to shelter himself in. It seems unlikely to me that my father was the whole interest of his parents. My father told me only two stories about his own father in his entire life. The first was the one about eating the cervelat sausage and jelly sandwiches at building sites —

a nice, nostalgic story. The kind of old-fashioned thing that father and son pals could do in the old days. The second was the story of my grandfather on his deathbed, giving my grandmother instructions on my father's upbringing. "He's too slight for carpentry," he said, "But he's smart. Let him go into drafting."

This story was double-edged. On the one hand, it showed my grandfather's ferocious devotion, plotting out my father's future, as he lay dying of lung cancer in 1926, probably without anything to ease the pain. It also conveys shame: my father was slight. He could not carry bricks and lumber all day, lift beams, build with his two hands. He would not carry on the family line, as his father and grandfather had: "William turned his hand to the trade of carpentry and established his two sons, Joseph and William Jr., in the trade with him as they grew up." But these two short stories were told over and over, as if we had never heard them. We listened politely every time. No other hints about his father were offered, except that my grandfather knew one saying in Czech that translated to "Kiss me, pretty girl." I was never shown a picture of him, never told more.

It seems now that there must have been other stories that my father held back from us, if his entire presentation of my grandfather amounted to the same two stories. He never showed us a picture of my grandfather, and we assumed that he had none. My father had said that losing him when he was fourteen was the worst thing that ever happened to him. Once he mentioned that at age forty or fifty, he still had dreams where his father reappeared. He said he never expected to live past his fifties, any longer than his father had. So perhaps the lost father had to be kept tight, inside a couple of nostalgic stories. Maybe he had been a wonderful father, and it was his early death that wiped out all the other stories. Maybe my grandfather was the easygoing rapscallion my father portrayed, the "onetime gold miner, hotel keeper, calla-lily picker, and carpenter." This was what my father seemed to want us to think. Maybe there were other reasons why my father told us so little.

AFTER my father's death, my brother and I went through the family pictures and saw a few pictures of my grandfather for the first time. He wasn't a gray, withered old man. Not a hammer-in-the-pocket, I'm-around-the-corner, your-neighbor-Mr.-Fixit kind of guy. He looked like a bounder. Posed for a picture, but thumbing his nose at the camera. He's holding a stogie in one hand, and looking at the camera, eye to eye, with some contempt, like the boy who's about to topple his chair in the classroom. In a picture with my father, the images are even more confusing. He and my father wear "good" clothes, shrunken-looking suit jackets, white shirts, knickers and a cap for my father, age nine or so, a sat-on-looking hat for his father. They're posing in the treeless backyard, the city kind, a little lot bounded by a wooden fence, with a view to the next yard and fence, and the next, and the next. There's a narrow alley between their yard and the house that lets out onto the front sidewalk. My grandfather is clowning. He stands aloof, far from my father, and aims his finger toward the top of my father's hat, as if my father were just a toy at the end of a beanie that my grandfather could spin on his finger. His pose seems to point out that my father is certainly the smaller one, not a man, or maybe not even his son, just some skinny kid from down the street who happened to pose with him. After the picture is over, maybe he'll disappear down the alleyway, down the street, or down to the corner for a quick one.

In my father's essay, his father is the "gallant" Bohemian, and my father was his "whole interest in life." But maybe he was a bounder, someone who stayed around just long enough to cast a shadow over the skinny child standing next to the backyard fence. My father had never shown us the pictures. Maybe they showed a man who viewed his own image, in the camera, with contempt, and the image of himself, in the face and body of his "slight" son, with contempt as well.

My father's claim that "indulgent" parents had given him a "superiority" complex seems suspect as well. The superiority he names clearly mirrors its opposite: "The first grade of school brought ... a barrier that has never been completely surmounted, that of friendly relations, with the average child, or man, or woman. The very bad, the very good, each awoke a responsive chord within me; but the average person has always been a source of annoyance to me." The Wizard of Oz, we find, the loud-speaking boss, who liked to boast how he roasted his secretary at work, or lambasted a "college boy" trainee, who criticized my mother about the thickness of pork chops, who flew up the stairs in a rage after his son, who called his daughter a "witch" when she complained about being ignored, who did not think it worth his time to stop to talk with a next-door neighbor, who ordered food imperiously from busy waitresses, the boy with the "superiority" complex, the Wizard, was still the skinny, hesitant boy, dwarfed and belittled by his father, pushed and nagged by his mother, standing "for hours" at a blackboard at age four. What he really suffered from was the painful distance between himself and those in the same room. Somehow, the connection had been severed early in his life, and he didn't know how to get it back, by age six, or by age fourteen, or by age twenty-one.

My father found ways to make more distance, to start traveling, to move from the middle field of daily life. From his hand in his child's, from a conversation with the butcher, from the house that he lived in, from the warm side of his wife, from the food on his own table. All yielded less to him than he needed. About "average" people, he continued: "I cannot make myself agreeable to them. Their smug, narrow security invariably provokes my contempt and criticism. Consequently, friends were few, and my loneliness has increased through the years." Reading this, I wondered if my father was just going through an I-am-different-from-mankind phase common to twenty-year-olds, or if this scorn was a part of him that took root in many disguises. A photograph of him in Harlem at a party, in 1946, shows him looking above the crowd. The way someone looks out on rooftops from another rooftop. Maybe trying to mingle, at the edges, with a bourbon and a cigarette attached to his hand. As a newly married husband in 1942, he poses at home with his bride. They're dressed up. She wears a flowered dress with a prim lace collar. He wears a suit, but he's still skinny and he doesn't fit into the shoulders. They sit tightly in the center of the couch, directly below a mantelpiece, where a vase of stiff flowers sits in the center. He looks shell-shocked, stunned, like a deer caught by headlights, afraid that someone will find him out for not really being a grown-up, with his baggy shoulders. Twenty years later, posing for a publicity picture as the vice president of a machine company, he's gained weight, is maybe even a bit too portly. He looks substantial, but still cannot look straight into the camera.

The twenty-one-year-old writer claims that life got better. By the age of sixteen, he was becoming competent in mechanical drawing and found that he could "absorb" himself in it. This would have been a relief for the in-love-with-long-distance man. He picked out a hothouse group of friends by "cultivating my favorite tastes and choosing my associates accordingly" but added that "my clashes with the average man and woman still continue." And perhaps that was his problem as a family man as well — we were only "average," and the family idea was only "average."

EVEN before we read his essay, my brother and I knew my father was a boy underneath. So we protected him. It prevented us from getting really mad at him. How could you pick on this skinny kid?

It was as if we were the parents, who didn't want to hurt the child's feelings, to blow his cover when he put on big shoes, a hat, and carried an oversized briefcase. It was tricky. We were also children, and wanted to feel that we had an actual grown-up, not a masquerading grown-up, for a father. We had to travel quite a distance ourselves to train ourselves not to be there, in order to tolerate being there, only shadow people. Where were we? I was Fern, bringing her pig to the state fair in Kansas. Or a Russian brain surgeon in Moscow. Or the writer of many novels, like Margery Sharp, sitting in my second-story pied-à-terre. Or in a novel with a tumultuous setting, like *Britannia Mews* or *Jamaica Inn.* My brother was out in the field behind our house, digging a hole in the ground named "Alabama" that was bigger than his bedroom. My sister was sitting at her glass-topped vanity table dreaming about a boy putting a pendant around her neck. My mother seemed to drift out the window of whatever room surrounded her. It is true that my mother, father, sister, brother, and I ate together at a table without being there at all. This became our story.

Traveling Man

WE lived in a house by a field on the outskirts of a Midwestern city, but my father lived in St. Paul, Los Angeles, Detroit, Louisville, Wheeling, Milwaukee, Santa Fe, and Toronto as well, in and out, on a weekly basis. More occasionally, he took longer trips to England, Cuba, or Denmark. He was a traveling man. He visited breweries and soft-drink plants, to check the washer and spider valves and pasteurizers on the machines he designed and sold. These were room-sized machines that put many bottle caps on per minute, rinsed out two thousand brown beer bottles in an hour, or fixed a piece of cork to the caps of soda bottles. He did business, had lunch, had drinks, went out to dinner. He roamed streets, always wanting the time to find the little store at the corner that had special white sausages, or a loaf of sourdough bread, sometimes finding it, bringing home a string of sausages from Milwaukee in his suitcase, putting them on our table, or a very large grapefruit from California, or a sheaf of unused labels from the Pearl Brewery with a picture of a beautiful ram, to use as scrap paper. By the time I was old enough to know, the routine of his absence was a fact of our household. He was coming, or going, but seldom simply there.

"I was never so happy as when the train wheels started to turn under me," he once said with a great deal of relish, when I was grown and he was old. As if I were supposed to happily congratulate him, and say yes, you were a traveling man, that species of now-

you-see-him, now-you-don't male. He seemed unaware that a traveling man left some blank spots behind. This was the father who
couldn't remember your friends' names, didn't know what was in
your birthday present, wasn't in the auditorium. There were many
other things I wished that he might have said, like "I was never so
happy as the first time I held you in my arms," or "I was never so
happy as when we walked in the field behind our house," or "I was
never so happy as watching you dig in the mud by the gully," that
would have been about connection, not train wheels and distance.

So the image of my father's suitcase, lying on the bed, opened,
illuminated by the seemingly innocent northern sunlight of 1950s
suburban St. Louis, the white pressed shirts shining like paper,
comes to stand for much of my ambivalence toward this traveling
man. The suitcase was a wonder, with its scent of leather, tobacco,
freshly starched shirts, and shoe polish. It was also the instrument
of exchange. With his suitcase, we traded our father for the life his
trips garnered: the good clothes, the mother who didn't work, the
dustless house, the polished mahogany dining-room table, the good
pediatrician, the education paved solidly to college. A life without
hasty surprises, as his had been. So the instrument of exchange was
carefully prepared. One of my mother's jobs was to make sure its
components were there, the shirts home from the cleaner, the gold-
toe socks matched and balled, a carton of Pall Malls, a fifth of
bourbon, three pairs of shoes polished, covered with something that
looked like socks so they didn't get scuffed. Two pairs of cufflinks,
one square, one round, enough shorts and sleeveless undershirts,
some pajamas with piping that looked like Cary Grant's, a traveling
alarm clock with a face that glowed.

The open suitcase filled me with a mixture of dread, curiosity,
and envy. I hated the fact that my father was leaving, once again,
and we would wrench ourselves back to adjust to his absence. Without him, we ate little cozy meals of beans and franks in the kitchen

with my mother, not having to sit politely at the dinner table and fidget during his long narrations about spider valves and ball bearings. No one to yell at you for forgetting to make ice cubes again to chill his martini. This was good. But also, without him, there was no one to jump on at six o'clock, no one to sit me in his lap and read the comics to me, particularly "Nancy," although it was never funny. No one to play horse, or to run the dog in the field, or play a game where he put me on his shoulders, and I looked into a mirror as we walked around, and it seemed as if I was walking on the ceiling. No jokes, no tricks. My father represented change, and other lives. My mother was stasis, the low simmering routines of the day.

So the open suitcase shut. When it returned with my father, there was a certain amount of fanfare to look forward to. Getting ready to go to the airport. Phone calls from my mother to my grandmother about arrival time. Leaving the house so we wouldn't be late, moving the cat and dog in or out of the house. Lambert Airport was as much a part of my childhood routine as Kroger's Supermarket or Schmidt's Bakery. When we got there, my mother and I waited for the silvery plane to come in, searching the windows for my father's profile. He had many gold teeth, and we would say that you could see them glinting in the sun, in the window, so that's how we could find him. Getting off the plane, coming down the staircase, he struck the standard profile of a fifties traveling man: overcoat with raglan sleeves, felt fedora, leather accordion briefcase, wing-tip shoes. He seemed thrilled to see me again, after being gone. My daily reunions with my mother, who never got to go anywhere, made no particular mark.

We'd take my father home, and my older brother and sister would get home from school. My mother would have gotten the ingredients for a meal he particularly liked, usually involving a pork chop and some potatoes. We'd eat at the mahogany table in the dining room again and he'd tell us about his evening having beer and sauerbraten in Milwaukee, of a particularly fine piece of ham and pie in West Virginia, or about tracking down an old bakery on a side street in St. Paul when he found himself with nothing to do for a few hours in the morning. And more about the spider valves, the ball bearings, the bottle caps, the pasteurizer, Mr. Strogiano or Mr. Chandler or Mr. Weatherwax or Mr. Weiss or Mr. Busch, the big men of the beer world. In that suitcase, there'd be something for us, Callard & Bowser butterscotch from Canada, or the gum from the airplane, or a tiny plastic Coca-Cola bottle from a bottling plant, a pack of cards with pictures of machinery on the back, some special macaroons. So in exchange for giving him up, we got irresistible hints about the mysteries of even the most plain-faced of American cities, Detroit, Louisville, or St. Paul. He said their names with reverence, as if he were speaking of a wise, complex old sage. There seemed to be so many alluring cities on the American continent, each with an endless supply of secret streets, untasted by us. Newark, Milwaukee, Santa Fe, Tallahassee. The trains that rambled toward them were certainly the same thing as destiny. And our father, on those trains, was fulfilling destiny.

MY father was a traveling man, it was said. The kind of man who liked to travel, the way a drinking man liked to drink. Later I would realize that a drinking man is always a traveling man, whether he actually goes anywhere or not. For many years, I thought the long yearning I felt about my father was the result of his being on the road so much. I wanted him to be around more, like the fathers in television families. Somehow, whenever Beaver blew it, Ward was conveniently located in his study, available to have one of those stern but kindly, reassuring and clarifying chats with Beaver. Or Fred MacMurray was off in his den smoking a pipe, and ready to lend an ear if one of his boys developed a crush on the wrong girl, or if someone made fun of his glasses at school. Of course, there was *Father Knows Best,* with the irreproachable Robert Young calling his youngest girl "Kitten," and stopping dead in his tracks if she needed a little heart-to-heart talk, with his indispensable "best" advice. My favorite fantasy dad was John Forsyth as *Bachelor Father,* I suppose because his orphaned niece got him all to herself, as they drove off gaily in a convertible.

From my own experience, from many conversations with friends my age, and from my own reading, I know of nothing that remotely supports this TV fantasy of physically available, emotionally tuned-in fathers in the 1950s. The more common picture is remote — he could be traveling for work, or he could be obsessed with his work at the office or the lab. He could be at home, but with extra work to make more money, so he was hidden in the basement at night. Maybe he had some mounting interest in being down at the corner, at a bar or club. There was the idea of being a good father by making as much money as possible. This took time. There was also the idea, as in my father's case, of making a clearly middle-class life for himself and his children. The sacrifice of his presence, if indeed he felt it to be a sacrifice ("I'm happiest when the train wheels turn underneath me"), was simply what was needed to secure his new place.

That a family might be frayed by the father's work was clearly less important than bettering oneself — as in the phenomenon of being "transferred" for business. The idea that a father might refuse a better job across the country because his family would be uprooted, because his wife would leave her mother and aunts, her children their grandparents and cousins, was viewed as perhaps old-fashioned. Families were ties that bound, and a traveling man needed to move on. Beaver's dad or the father who knew best might have turned down a job so their boys could keep delivering papers down the same street, so their daughters could call up the same friends on the telephone. But no father I knew of ever would have made such a choice, certainly not mine. When we moved east, we stayed in a furnished apartment, a dreary place that doubled as a motel, while our new house was readied. In the hallway, I sat on the floor and played jacks with Mary from across the hall. She was in the hallway for the same reason I was — her father had been transferred. It was something like having a barbecue; a lot of families did it.

We were the first generation to be engaged in this daily mind game with the TV, constantly comparing our experience with what appeared on the screen. There were many, many shows depicting warm, close-knit families rollicking through the ups and downs of daily life together, always with problems addressed and resolutions reached by the end of the half hour. What was TV, anyway? I was at least in my teens before I realized that it was fabrication and fantasy. As a child, I viewed it as some kind of index, or documentation, of real life, as lived elsewhere, and maybe even as lived in my own house, my own living room. Wasn't my father, bursting through the door in a white shirt at 6:00 P.M., just like the father on *Father Knows Best?* I am sure part of my idea of my father, and mother, depended upon the superimposition of the constant, chronic TV image on my own daily experience, like a filter that changed an average homecoming at 6:00 P.M. to the perfection of the TV moment. The mother, in a crisp apron, hair rolled perfectly, delighted at the father's return. The little daughter running to the door. The older son, a bit adolescent and awkward, but forward-looking, happy to have his father home, so his father can help out with the airplane he is building in the basement. The older daughter, pretty as a picture, hair swept back, demure in her angora sweater and ponytail, ready to get his view on her upcoming election as class secretary.

In the ideal TV family, the mothers were never going crazy from boredom, or intellectual restlessness, or a lack of conversation. They loved making sandwiches and waiting for their children to run through the kitchen. The fathers were never crabby from working too much, never resentful that their wives and children enjoyed their beauteous suburban house while they commuted to work and ingratiated themselves with the boss, never smoldered from work and routine. The children did not hesitate to share their little joys and sorrows with their parents, who were always willing to drop everything and listen and offer a tactful solution. This was the safe, routine life, after the war, and the bomb.

TV was a bromide, a balm. Now we know that fathers felt trapped, mothers resentful, children silenced and fearful. This was not discussed, in little chats, or elsewhere, until many years later. It was chaotically and indirectly discussed in the upheavals of the 1960s, painstakingly and privately discussed with individuals in therapy, broadly discussed in the family-as-system movement, and in various kinds of laymen's recovery movements. Now we can speculate about what force drove so many TV scriptwriters to insist that families were open, communicative, problem-solving units, and what hunger drove so many hypnotized American adults and children to participate in this ritual insistence. TV was something to fool children with, and their parents, as well.

IT took me almost thirty years to realize that even if my father had been sitting in his study, smoking a pipe, he would not have been able to come forth with the little chat. Such intimacy made him anxious. He looked like he wanted the next train to come. Being a drinking man as well as a traveling man put him off in some zone where he couldn't be reached. Anything of an interior nature was like a tornado coming through. Better to turn out the lights and go down to the basement. He would look apologetic and embarrassed at the same time. Someone made fun of your glasses?

I suppose, now, he didn't know any more than we did about this, and as the father who was under pressure to know best, he felt ashamed that he didn't. So he would be evasive, or laugh a little, or be dismissive. "Oh, piffle," he might say. No help here. Family life, in general, I think made him nervous, with all its demands for patience, and its emotional ambiguities. Not always knowing the right thing, and not being able to save your children, always, from the same humiliations you had suffered. And there was the effort to let go of his own world, and enter into the little dramas of his children's lives. It was too much.

Yet, he was extremely attached to the idea of himself as a family man. It is true that he loved us, without being very good at what followed. He also seemed to need the image of his tidy home, clean children, docile wife behind him, so he could present the right picture of himself to the business world. He liked to think of himself as an exceptional parent. He told the leader of the Ethical Culture Society once that he and my mother took their parenting seriously. But he could not see the distance between what he thought he was doing and what actually happened in our home. It went like this: Walk in the door at 6:00 P.M., crack the ice, make the martinis. Toss the smallest child around a bit, say hello to the big ones. Get spaced out, in this little hive full of people who need you to play baseball on the vacant lot, to read a bedtime story, to listen to a mother's hopes and fears at midnight. Another martini. Narrate the story of your day on the job; no need to question the children or the mother about their day. Pull some papers out of your briefcase.

We played along. We cast our father as the martini-and-ciga-rette, time-to-go-out-the-door kind of father, like William Powell in *The Thin Man,* not the cardigan-wearing, have-a-chat, let's-check-out-your-project-in-the-basement kind of father.

He hadn't been in the door more than five minutes when the ice cracked. There was a sinking feeling, as there was about his suitcase, as soon as you heard that crack. I did not remember the sinking feeling until about thirty years later. I remembered it only as a routine household sound, like coffee perking in the morning, or a dog barking before its dinner. My older brother tells me that when he was little, my mother complained about the martini ritual. By the time I observed it, seven years later, it was merely a fact of household life. Not a ripple of disturbance. My mother had given up, I suppose, fallen further into the ivy-twined wallpaper, in her long sigh of resignation.

So my father, the traveling man, actually began traveling again the minute he walked in the door. In a basic way, he could not stand to be where he was, ever. When I was a child, I thought the problem was that he couldn't stand to be with us. I see now that merely being inside of his own skin, simply being there, triggered some kind of panic in him that sent him looking across the horizon for the nearest train. I am sure there were reasons. For years I thought it was the Depression. He learned how to look out for himself like an alley cat, learned too well maybe, and then became like an alley cat who couldn't sit still for domestic life.

Then I read other people's accounts of living through the Depression. Hardship, yes, everywhere, but not always bitterness. I realized that this bitterness, the broken chip, the unfulfilled prom- ise, the need to be buffered by other people's impressions, the desire for escape, was a temperamental thing with my father, not part of every survivor of that decade. It was something he had learned.

I picture my father at sixteen, the man of the house for two years now, going up on the roof of the machinery company. His mother is at home worrying, or cooking his supper, or thinking about his lost sister with the wavy hair. His hands are in his pockets. The other boys in the office are there too, but he feels alone. He's not really good at horsing around with them. He's better at finding train yards, or warehouses, or clouds that look like tornadoes from above, by himself. He smokes, like they do. When it's time to go home, to the flat on Penrose Street, he walks to save carfare. He stops in the park, pulls something from his pocket. A piece of paper. Something he's written the night before, a poem, or an outraged letter to the editor. Something he thinks sounds very fine. Men in damp coats everywhere are going home for dinner. He stays there, with his piece of paper in his hand.

MAYBE this alley cat never got to learn the essentials of being with others. Maybe he was exchanged too early for the wages he could earn, and felt robbed. It was hard for him to ask on a daily basis, "How are you?" He usually did not take the initiative. It was harder still for him to listen to the answer. He'd fidget, look off in another direction, answer the sound of whatever inner call he had. So he suffered, too, in loneliness. He had hurt many people's feelings, many, many times, as when he forgot to ask his children and wife daily how they were. He was baffled in later years when people left him, moved across the country, forgot his birthday, didn't answer his letters.

When I was in high school, on a dreary February day, I remember the floor nearly seeming to fall out from me when we read *The Glass Menagerie*. The father had deserted the family. He worked for the telephone company, and, as Amanda, the mother, tartly says, "was in love with long distance." I knew this deeply. But the man in the play, I kept telling myself, had really gone. He left them there broke, and the son was stuck in the shoe factory. My hardworking father couldn't be the same. Yet I realize now that my father, and many other hardworking, ambitious, traveling and drinking men of the 1950s, and other times as well, had a different kind of disappearing act altogether. They didn't leave, as the father in the

Glass Menagerie did. But they were in love with long distance. They stayed, but they were not there. They maintained their own house, with its own rules and language, unknown to their wives and children. Their wives were upset, but felt they had no recourse. Perhaps the mothers yelled at their children too much, or did not talk to them, or were so grateful to be kept in a house that they did not think to want more. And so it was that the leafy arms of maple trees lining the streets seemed the most reliable, and welcoming, of all.

WHEN my father died, there was a moment in the funeral service when my brother and I simultaneously seemed to acknowledge that he was finally gone. We are angry and surprised. There was always a tolerance we had had to develop, sort of a permanent excuse, for having a father who was there, but not there, a constantly traveling man. You knew he couldn't do much better. You knew he looked as if he'd die if he were going to have to sit down and have that talk with you. We knew he was not that sort of man. But we couldn't stop waiting for him to turn into one — thirty years, forty years.

If wishes were horses, beggars would ride. Every day, this wish. Come back, and stay. And now he was certainly, finally, beyond our reach, gone on what seemed, for a moment, just another business trip, the suitcase all locked up. It was the end of the wishes. Now we could never make him come back, from St. Paul, from the vague places of his imagination, from the spider valves.

I had carried a fantasy that there was one solid thing I could do that would stop my father, really make him look at me. For some reason I always pictured it as my first book, that he could hold it in his hands, some weight there, or a new child of mine in his arms. But he was always hard to pin down. When I called to tell him that my first child was just born, my perfect new girl, he was clearly stunned. I had stopped him for a minute. But he was a resilient street cat, after all, and landed back on his feet. "I am transported," he said, and I knew years later that it was giving him transport, more than the solid baby, that made me a good daughter at that moment.

A few months after he died, I seemed to be walking on a tide of grief that knew no reason. I walked through town on a hot day. I stopped suddenly on the pavement. A freight train suddenly broke through the center of town. The beautiful colors, the beautiful names. Red for Santa Fe, green for Maine, yellow for Louisville, rusty brown for Canadian National. That train had to have been my father, I thought. He was transported, I was transported, he was sending me the message of those rambling tracks and the beautiful names of cities. Now, writing, I hear a train off in the distance, and the old mixture of sadness and joy cuts through me: parting, and reunion; distance, and hope of joining.

Those trains still break my sleep. They will never stop reminding me of Midwestern tracks that leap forward and back to Minneapolis, or Detroit, or St. Paul, with the suitcase full of five starched shirts, shining like paper. Hope and longing. And this is what the word "father" has come to mean to me as well, as if, finally, he was a metaphor, or a medium, for transport itself. He took me here to earth, and left me to figure this out.

From him, I learned about the value of transport, how finding the perfect word could lift you. A sinister metaphor always made him happy: "Cold as a hog on ice," he'd say, and wait until we saw it. He was the one who took me into a field and told me the wondrous names of plants, Queen Anne's lace, sumac, pokeweed, sassafras. I learned about the value of being in transport, of finding a fresh beer in Prague. Some swans in the water in Denmark. A dusty bakery in Chicago. A large possum staring in a field. I am not sure yet what it means, to learn transport, from a father, rather than something about presence. When he died, a wise person said to me, "Your father will be with you more in death than he was in life." I see now that she might be right, in more ways than she knew.

Can Opener

WHEN my father fixed a faucet, the whole household and the whole day was rearranged around this event. Fixing the leaky faucet involved a long windup: having a second cup of coffee, a cigarette, going down into the basement, which was full of old golf balls and sow bugs. Then he dragged out his tools from under his workbench, and his dead father's tools and maybe even his dead father-in-law's old dental tools. I liked to follow him around. I saw him so rarely during the week that tagging after him for even the most boring of procedures seemed like a privilege. And he was in his preferred element — with tools, puffing on a Pall Mall, looking for a solution, disgusted when a washer didn't fit, having to make numerous pro- tracted trips to the hardware store, stopping for a well-earned beer, shouting all over different parts of the house to shut off the water here or to try it there, to see if it was working. Being the boss. Maybe I'd even get to hold something for him, a wrench or a bolt. I was the only girl I knew who could hammer a nail straight. Then, when it was nearly dinnertime on a Saturday, the job finally done to his satisfaction, he'd say what he'd always say: "You'd better marry an engineer, so you can get things fixed the right way around the house."

And so it was that one of the last and most important presents my father made to me was mechanical as well — a can opener with a lifetime guarantee. He was visiting me in Brooklyn. I was twenty- nine, he was sixty-nine. I lived in a long skinny apartment, with bull's-eye molding at the corners of windows and doors, and claw feet on the bathtub. I was trying to be a scholar, and a poet, alternately writing about Emily Dickinson and pizzerias in Brooklyn. I had a part-time job in the library of the Fashion Institute of Technology, helping students find articles in magazines like *Footwear on Parade* and *Fur Weekly.* Roger, the man I lived with, was getting occasional free-lance jobs in television productions and working as a cook in bars and restaurants. Like everyone else we knew, we were becoming something, and doing something else in the meantime, or so we thought. We were trying to beat the rap, on our way to making some kind of extraordinary life, some indelible impression on the landscape. Maybe we weren't really doing anything, except hanging out and finding the cheapest plate of lo mein in Chinatown.

I don't know what my father thought about my life at the time. Maybe he thought, well, my daughter is really on the right track here. Or maybe he thought, her life seems marginal, alarming, misguided, but I won't let her know that I think that. The only slightly worried comment he made was about my apartment. It was a floor-through flat that had windows at the front and at the back, with two small windowless rooms in the middle. These perplexed and distressed him a bit. "We were poor, when I was young," he said, "but we always had rooms with windows."

But for the most part, he seemed extremely pleased with himself on these visits to Brooklyn. He was now old and in poor health. He was living a mostly housebound life, without the latitude and escape of his forty years as a traveling businessman. When he got on the train to come up and visit me, he was purely happy just to be moving, and also purely happy to be able to have a few beers in peace. And I suppose happy to have a daughter on the other end who humored him, fussed a bit about his health and smoking and drinking, but never called him out.

In the Brooklyn years, he arrived in pretty good shape, despite having had a stroke and repair work on his arteries. He insisted on taking the subway. This was perilous, since you have to get off and on fairly quickly, and his perception of how quickly he moved was out of synch with real time. He was so courtly that he would not take a seat on the train if there was only one. He gave it to me. When we got to Brooklyn, he'd send me out for beer or wine, as if it was a festive thing that any girl would want to have in her house for a visiting relative. There was most likely a pint of Old Crow in his suitcase, the one a friend of mine dubbed Old Businessman. Which is what my father would have been happy to be known as.

During these visits, my father and I caught up with each other. He'd ask some fatherly questions about my job, and more pointedly about Roger's job. He had decided to like Roger a long time ago and always seemed to view any one of his jack-of-all-trades job roles — stockbroker, video producer, cook, teacher — as a promising start to a stellar career like his own. My work to him was a source of pride, but ultimately had less weight. He still wanted to feel that I would be "taken care of," as he had promised himself to do when I was small, so many times. He knew that I wanted to have my own work, and did not expect to be taken care of. But he still wished for it. I once visited him two days after I had a bicycle accident. I had been knocked unconscious, hit on the head, couldn't remember my phone number, had a little gravel and many bruises on my face. When Roger and I got out of the car, he inspected my black-and-blue head critically and said, quickly, severely, to Roger, "You're not taking care of her."

However, whose job this was — taking care of me — was never particularly clear. It was my father's stated belief and intent, when I was a child, that I "would always be taken care of." This was understood to mean two things. First, that he would always be successful enough in business so that I would be provided for. Nice clothes, no worries, straight to college. Second, that I would marry a man of sufficient moral and professional caliber that I would not "have" to work, a man who would take care of me.

Being "taken care of" meant, for my father and for many other men of his generation, financial support and whatever emotional stability resulted from having enough money not to worry. It did not mean, for example, really tackling the reason why his daughter, who had wanted to be a doctor, was dating a part-time heroin user in high school and thinking about dropping out. Taking care of me did not mean making me sandwiches, or meeting my teachers or my friends' mothers, or polishing my shoes. It did not mean learning how to do these things when I was eleven and my mother died, or taking a job that involved less travel so that he could learn. It did not mean letting me sit in his lap and cry every night for a year about my dead mother. It meant making money, succeeding at an exceptional job, and fixing leaky faucets very, very carefully.

Okay. So I hadn't married an engineer, or anyone else who looked like he'd be able to take care of me. I hadn't married anyone yet. He'd had to take it on my word that Roger, whom I'd lived with since I was nineteen, was not the philandering sort. He could sort of fix a faucet, was smart in many other ways, and always seemed to be on the brink of a promising career. And was loyal to me. It seemed to be enough for my father, who said that he'd only worried about me once, when I'd dropped out of college, and gone off to live on the farm in New Hampshire. So two of my rooms had no windows. He enjoyed his visits. We took him around the city. He'd always been able to pick out a good detail, and there were corners of his vision that still worked. He'd make us stop to look at columns and cornices on cast-iron buildings in Soho. When we took him to Chinatown to eat a dish with tiny ears of corn and red peppers in it he said, with all the happiness of one who loved to eat in strange places, "Look at those beautiful little ears!" One day he took two and a half hours' worth of hot subway trains so he

could admire the engineering of the tramway to Roosevelt Island.
He insisted on going himself, and the clock in my kitchen seemed
frozen until he returned.

I would play good daughter, listen to his stories, and make popovers
for breakfast, or find the special white sausages he liked with red
cabbage. There was not much he could do to take care of me any
longer. His health had collapsed when I was in college, so I'd finished putting myself through college and now graduate school. I'd
lived with the same man for ten years. I was younger, and now
physically stronger, and could see better. The other kinds of taking
care of, the listening and being-with and sandwich-making ones, he
had improved at a bit, now that he was old and ill, and couldn't
leave for work or escape to the basement to pick up his drafting
pencil. But they still made him nervous.

I only had enough nerve to ask him to stop drinking once. It
didn't work, and I thought repeated attempts would just result in
more fog. He'd retreat and ignore me. He would quietly refuse my
invitations to Brooklyn. Somehow I believed that our lifelong
deception — his falling into taxicabs and not even mentioning it,
stocking my refrigerator with cheap wine, and telling me when to
comb my hair, and my humoring him along — was keeping him
alive. I see now that we spent so much of the time avoiding any
problem that did not have a practical solution that I began to equate
telling the truth with dissolution.

SO you can see how happy it made my father, and me, when he
found one clear way to take care of me, when I was twenty-nine
and living a would-be life on a muzzy street in Brooklyn. He watched
me one evening as I was struggling to open a can of tomatoes with
an unreliable can opener, almost cutting my fingers on the jagged
edges — a thought which seemed to cause him more physical pain

than it did me. And I was not getting on with my daughter's job of fixing dinner. This was it, then. He could fix it: he'd buy me a new can opener. A clear, mechanical, finite solution.

We were all happy about this idea. It gave us a clear goal. Roger knew that the best hardware stores in the city were on Canal Street. My father knew what kind of can opener he wanted. We made a special trip into the city to buy a can opener and eat dinner in Chinatown, the idea festive in and of itself. We walked together along the noisy street, full of toys from Taiwan that would break in a minute, spare parts for window fans, camouflage pants from the army, spiky dog-collar arm bands, industrial-sized rolls of copper wire, used pedestal sinks, old telephones. There were at least ten hardware stores. My father selected the most promising, and we sent him in there by himself, to browse to his heart's content.

I thought he might die in the hardware store. It was hot, and he seemed a bit intoxicated with his sense of mission. He was wearing a T-shirt, which put him at a disadvantage these years because he was scrawny and his skin had a weather-beaten tone. When I was little, I thought he was part Indian. Then I thought it was sunburn. But it was years of drinking, alcohol flush. He met us across the street, looking hot and satisfied. "Here," he said. "I found just what I was looking for." Well, at last. It was gratifying to have him perfectly satisfied, if only for a moment. We came home and tried it out on a can of beans. It was pronounced a success.

And for several months it was, but then this can opener with the lifetime guarantee began to go awry. It leaped off the track of the lip of the can. It cut through parts of the lid and skipped others. For a while it worked if you held it and the can together up in the air. Then that trick failed, and you could sometimes get it to work by bearing down very hard. Then that stopped working. The best you could get was the lid opened about halfway with jagged edges, the kind you were warned about gravely when you were a child. It had happened to me, then, that fate that should always be avoided — jagged edges on a can. But I worked out a technique. With a great deal of patience, you could go over and over the skipped parts, and get about half the lid completely cut through. You had to watch out for little sharp shards of tin falling into the food, though. Then you stuck a knife in the can, and wedged up the free half of the lid, so that at least the beans or tomatoes could get out. It was not the proper way to open a can. My father the engineer would have cringed, had he been watching.

This can opener certainly cost less than five dollars, and even on my student budget, I think I could have gone out and bought a new one. I used it all through Brooklyn. Took it with me to New Jersey, finished my dissertation, married Roger, had a baby, taught college at night, taught summer school, moved to a bigger apartment in New Jersey, carried it with me, drove to Albany for a job, made much, much spaghetti, chili, and tuna fish, on a daily basis. I went to Block Island with the baby, I finished the manuscript for my first book, I wrote more poems. I applied for lots of teaching jobs at gloomy Northeastern schools that I never got. I switched to free-lance writing. I had another baby, the book came out, I finally got a real teaching job, I made more spaghetti. I had a full house, and it was usually very exhausting.

One day during these years I had a vision of how to improve my life in a sweeping, radical way. Buy ready-made tomato sauce, as most of the less stubborn people in the United States did. Shafts of light surrounded this idea. I would have extra time to look out the window, read the newspaper, write poetry, or build towers on the floor with my child. The feeling of doing a bad job as a writer and a mother, of being in two places at once, would be over. I would be happy again. I decided to make a lasagna with the new sauce before I left for work in Albany. The baby and I took one of those brimming-with-expectancy baby-and-I walks down to the corner supermarket. I bought the best-looking jar of tomato sauce I could find, felt beatific, then nervous. I dropped the jar on the supermarket floor, shattering the glass, and took it as a sign I'd made a mistake. Now it was too late to fool around anymore if I was going to get to work in Albany on time. I abandoned the dinner plan. It was the day my father died, I found out later, and I felt certain it happened at the exact moment the jar of spaghetti sauce flew out of my hands.

So I continued struggling with the lifetime guarantee can opener. Now my father had been gone for a few years. I thought I had things in perspective. A lucky woman, two beautiful children, a book, a one-of-a-kind husband, and an interesting job. Only what it was really like at 5:00 P.M. was this: Feeling like dead trampled meat from being at work, speeding guiltily home on a six-lane highway with a "suicide" divider, finding no food waiting, and two hungry children milling around the kitchen and then more and more frantically circling around, a little crying, whining, *Mommee,* when we are eating, and I'm using the can opener, to feed my precious ones, opening up another can of tomatoes to start dinner too late anyway, then the children pressing at my legs and feet again. I'm standing there, about to open about a quarter inch of can at a time, using a knife to turn up the ragged edge, and suddenly realize that I could be about to cut myself, maybe on a big vein, give my children the ineradicable memory of their mother bleeding to death before their eyes, because she did not have enough sense to throw the old can opener away. I couldn't admit that it really didn't work, that so many of the things my father had left to me did not work, and maybe now they were killing me.

THIS moment of revelation was not enough, however. Many more months went by without my changing the can-opening situation. I

was used to it. I had a way of dealing with it. It was a little dangerous, but okay. Now I was officially "in recovery." I mean by this
that I had been in and out of various psychotherapies for years with
much help. But now I was going to a group sponsored by Alcoholics
Anonymous for the children of alcoholic families. My skin, it seemed,
had fallen off. I admitted my family had been chaotic, my life now
was chaotic, and I vowed that I would do all I could to overcome
this legacy.

Okay. I saw that the can opener had to go. There were so many
things that had to go, though. Like others at the beginning of
recovery, I was overwhelmed. Where to start? Phone up the collection agency? Change the oil in the car? Clean out the box room?
Rewrite my childhood? Understand why my child woke in the night?
Why I was enraged to wake in the night? Why the slightest problem
with my husband made me feel like the earth was opening up? Quit
my job, which seemed to make me as anxious as my father had
been? Leave my beloved Roger, since despite our best intentions,
we were turning into a couple you'd rather not know? Just about
everything seemed sick. It was then that I began waking in the
middle of the night, panic-stricken. It seemed that this person I had
built, the delicate, careful structure of the scholar and poet and
mother, of even the strong, hash-slinging survivor, the mate and
mother, was about to fall, scatter in pieces flat on the floor, blow
away when the floor fan turned its big metal blades in my direction.

But I found that recovery is a process with its moments of peace,
its sailboat days as well. Peculiar feelings of relief, clarity, calm,
even very ordinary calm, arrive unexpectedly. On one such day I
decided to take a walk to the corner with my children to go to the
store, another one of those dreamed-of walks to the corner now
with two children. One holds my hand with the absolute confidence
that I always find stunning. The other leans into my arms. I'm the
mother who watches out for cars, curbs, and hidden dogs. They are

the children holding large maple leafs in their hands, as if the earth had created those leaves, only and expressly, for them. So we do this ordinary thing. We go to the store to buy light bulbs, some twine, a new bib for the baby — something I find to be extraordinarily difficult, the practical, helpful gesture, to set up my house. But for this moment I am happy to be an ordinary person taking an ordinary walk, and while we're in the store, I buy a new can opener. It has white handles, and it works perfectly. Every time I use it, I can't believe how easy it could have been, all those years, to do the ordinary thing.

Future Perfect

WE always drove, and our starting point was always St. Louis, and the direction was east, north, or west. Not south, because it was even hotter, and because we never felt comfortable in the south, having defined ourselves according to the Czechoslovakian Nekola who signed himself up for the Union Army. This meant that in whatever direction we went, there were many hours, even days, of flat fields full of pigs or corn to cross. We measured time by the height of one cornfield or the next, whether the leaves were ruffled by a breeze. Crossing a river, that hard-to-find water, was a big event that our parents never let us ignore. My father usually had a few remarks about the style and construction of the bridge we were on, or the barges that made their progress down the river.

Our rivers, Missouri, Mississippi, Meramec. Our bridges, drawbridge, suspension, truss. Old Route 40, a three-lane highway, usually featured in these trips. I would trade much today just for an hour's time on Route 40, out in the middle of nowhere, the lower river valley basin part of Illinois, where the road became smoky as it tied down the rises on the hills. Where dark fields had just been plowed and new corn was growing, where a spotted gray horse stood meditatively at the top of a rise. Where wind was caught in windmills that didn't look too far removed from the pinwheels we built ourselves in school. The landscape was reduced to a few elements: tree, house, field, tractor, windmill. It looked like something we could build ourselves from a set of blocks, pull apart and assemble again, horse, hill, silo, road, all the signs of permanence and transience gathered together in unspeaking parts.

I wanted to be the same as that landscape and would tolerate many, many miles of deadly boring cornfields to find myself there. Silo, full of corn for the hogs. Field, full of corn for the silo. House, full of children to feed the pigs. Children, full of pies made by their mothers. Mothers, full of armloads of goldenrod and blackberries. Fathers, arms full of newborn calves or foals for the children. Children, gathered each night in quilts and long, long fields of corn.

I was just a suburban girl who knew nothing of why my own grandmother, the one who was said to have had horses but no shoes, had used all the iron in her body to get her husband to leave the farm and work in the city; why to her, the city was light, and this obscurity I so desired had many mean, muddy, and dark places that she had wanted to leave forever. So I held this landscape in my head, a place of supposed innocence, and let it be a resting place without a thought to the mud: tree, house, horse, road, barn. Someday I would arrive there, someday I would return there, the future perfect. This serene reverie of landscape was interrupted only by mysterious messages. If a farmer was too poor to paint his barn, he let a company that made chewing tobacco paint its roof or side as an advertisement. Three-story-high yellow-and-red letters spelled out "Mail Pouch Tobacco." I asked my parents about this incessantly. What was a mail pouch? Why would anyone want to chew tobacco? Spit it out? Plugs of tobacco seemed like old brown grasshoppers. They used to say that when you caught them in your hand they spit on you. More ennobling to the road were the red-and-white Burma-Shave signs, which gave you partial messages that eventually rhymed, something like "Toughest whiskers," and a few miles of cornfield later, "in the town," then a few more, "We hold them up," and then finally, "You mow them down — Burma-Shave."

They were something to look forward to, more like the TV and Cheez Doodle component of daily life than the litany of tree, field, horse, or the more severe message of the Mail Pouch Tobacco barn.

This was the time when my family seemed best able to approximate family life, vacation. My father sometimes tried to mix a little business in. There was a trip to Milwaukee that included a day when he stopped in on a brewery, and dinner at a rathskeller, known to those in the brewing industry, and a trip to Toronto when we stayed in a lodge for a few days while he checked out a bottling plant in town. But for the most part, he was more with us than usual, and good-humored; he was traveling at the same time. He was happy looking at maps, plotting out routes that would have us in a town like Chillicothe, Ohio, at lunchtime. He'd predict there'd be an old-style lunchroom there, with grooved water glasses that sweated, a menu typed up that day, a meat loaf special and fresh pie, served by a benevolent and aging waitress in a pink uniform, and he would usually be right.

My mother turned lighthearted as well. Her job, for a week or two, was no longer to be the stationary object, the keeper of our brick outpost on the field. She always packed sandwiches in waxed paper for the first day's lunch, and thoughtfully packed a little suitcase full of amusements for us, car lotto, cards, puzzles in frames. But after that she was freed. Or more free, at least. I would like to say she was totally freed, that she took to the wheel and took to the road, took us someplace that she longed to go, but my father was the captain of the ship. He planned the routes. He drove the car. She rode in front, provided sandwiches, amused the children, served as the relief driver, and read passages of historical interest from a WPA guidebook they usually took with them.

They did, however, agree on where to go and what to do together. Their trips usually fell into one of three categories: up north to a bungalow by the lake, out west for animals, to the east for culture.

Our earliest trips were to a family lodge up in Michigan, on the lake near Charlevoix. There really were rustling winds through the tall pine trees by the lake, bags of fresh cherries from a tiny stand by the road, sandy roasted hot dogs, and even a rainbow glimpsed out the back screen door, over the tops of trees. All five of us were there at once to see it. One year my father's boss let us use his Lake Michigan house. It was bigger than our house at home and had a broad lawn in front. There was a large old-fashioned kitchen inside, and my mother and sister were already talking about blueberry pancakes. We had taken my grandmother with us this time, since the house was so spacious, and she was happy to be involved in this new living room, in selecting a rattan chair by the fireplace. She had plenty of time to play cards with me, because now she didn't have to shuck peas or knead bread, or fret about the moth aunts or Uncle Ed.

The Everly Brothers were on the radio. I remember this because my sister was just getting old enough to take note of these things. The house was overrun with daddy longlegs spiders, and my brother invented a new form of torture for little sisters, chasing them with a daddy longlegs spider held by one leg. I seem to remember eating at a restaurant where they had pastries in the shape of a beautiful pink pig for dessert. On Lake Michigan, the water was lazy, good for floating with big black inner tubes. My brother specialized in sliding down dunes and my mother complained good-naturedly about sand in his clothes. My father got out his fishing tackle box and fixed up some lines with corks and weights for each of us, to dangle from the side of a boat, or off a dock.

It was not so hard to keep house in someone else's house, to eat around a table. We ate blueberry pancakes and bacon for dinner, happily, temporarily, in this house full of light from the lake, sand, and spiders. My mother put bundles of sweet peas and daisies in an old jar for the center of the table. There would be more vacation meals: Rice Krispies, from a tiny box, in a hotel in Toronto, where your breakfast milk came out of heavy little white jugs. Fried fish in South Dakota, that each of us had caught that day from a deep lake, perch, pike, catfish, all the children with their own fish. Scrambled eggs and bacon for breakfast on a farm in Arrowrock, Missouri, where we slept in feather beds and looked for arrowheads. A pecan pie in Wheeling, West Virginia. In between these times when we sat together stretched more roads with tree, horse, hill, and silo, held together with telephone wires. In these moments, we knew ourselves to be lucky, the children of a traveling man and his lovely accomplice with the history book, who were able to show us something about fixing the moving landscape.

Alabama

MY brother John's and my windows faced in the same direction, toward the side of the neighbor's house, over a quince bush. So my brother got the idea of having our own telephone line. This required two empty orange juice cans and a piece of string. We punched a hole in the bottom of each can, pushed the string through, and tied a big knot. Then my brother went outside to catch one end and I ran to his room to catch it when he threw it back up. This is the kind of thing my brother helped me to do. He taught me many practical skills of childhood. How to walk by a barking dog, very coolly, so it wouldn't bite you. How to fix a bowl of cornflakes, milk poured on first, then sugar, so the sugar wouldn't fall off. How to drain spit out of a trombone. How to scratch a sassafras root, so it would smell like root beer. How to tune in a primitive transistor radio shaped like a rocket. How to practice the broad jump by drawing a line and jumping over it. How to wash whitewalls, how to brush up leather shoes, how to get a finicky cat to sit on your lap, how to whistle.

I viewed my brother as knowledgeable on all subjects, and this was fortunate for both of us. My father often said that in the world of business, there would always be others trying to get ahead by "putting a knife in your back." Perhaps this is why the posture of father to son, to him, seemed to spring from a coil of fear. It translated to his constant, heedless criticism of his own son. Hammer it straight. It's only worth doing the right way. Take it out and do it again. Was he watching his back every moment? He did not see that this approach did not provide protection, just exposure. In the eye of my father's criticism, my brother could have no confidence about turning right or turning left, and often ended up, at that point, not knowing which way to go. Maybe my father felt that someone was constantly checking him, to see if he really was the father who knew best. His criticism was automatic, like breathing. My mother tried every now and then to break into this, but it was a system she couldn't crack. A kind of bad weather that moved in and pressed on us constantly. My sister was busy being the older sister, painting by numbers and fixing her hair. I consulted my brother often, about mud, dogs, how to get home, how to ride a bike, how fast to run. I was happy that my brother had elected himself to educate me in these areas.

MOURNING doves always started the summer, and cicadas always ended it. They were the refrain that marked the long summer days spent perfecting tin-can telephones, or paper airplanes, as my brother delivered me through time from his unformed tag-along little sister to a broad jumper and poker player as well. On summer evenings we sat at a card table on the back porch. It was dark and there was one lamp. We played Monopoly or poker, and my brother let me believe I was a whiz at either of these games. Raking up hotels on St. Charles or St. James Place, planting rows of profitable houses on the cheap but handy Baltic Street and Oriental Avenue. Making a big score for Ventnor, Marvin Gardens, handfuls of money. Or holding a hand full of good poker cards. The names themselves suggested plentitude. Flush. Full house. Or, mystery and escape. Jokers wild. Ace of spades. One-eyed jacks. We had a few disputes and consulted the *World Book Encyclopedia* awhile on poker to mediate.

Poker, right next to pokeweed, belladonna, rumored to be poisonous. Poker, rumored to be a game of poison, a game of ruin. My brother pretended to be surprised when I won. The monotonous assurance, like rain on a window, of these repetitive games, of knowing that here I could build a little city of houses or cards, or own a railroad for traveling, seemed to make our own house more solid. Full house. Pair of kings. You win again. Count the money. Ten hotels, two railroads, queen of hearts, high card wins. We built houses, we built cities. The cicadas took them away.

ONE summer the state built a highway through the vacant field behind our house, and my brother took his bike out every day to check on the progress. We hated the highway, because it cut up the field. But we loved the pipes, tunnels, and holes they dug to build it. But now there were fewer possums, since the main waterway, Stinky Creek, was dammed up. Lying in bed at night, behind the outline of the oak tree at the top of the hill, I saw hints of lights from the highway, headlight beams. Destinations, directions. The sound of trucks on the interstate became our constant companion as well. A truck winding itself up was intertwined with the mourning dove and cicada, but seemed to imply a further destination, a road, out, to be followed at some time. The distant glimmer and whine of the road finally became as friendly as the field before it.

WE lived in one house and built other ones all day long — tree houses, card houses, Monopoly board houses, doll houses. We walked into television houses every day, Ozzie and Harriet's, Desi and Lucy's, Ward and June's. Whatever deficiencies were present in our house were bound to be made up in theirs. These TV households seemed to be part of our own household, the more idealized version. It was not only the children who believed this. My two great-aunts, on a trip to California, had sent back a postcard of Ozzie and Harriet's house to my grandmother that said, "Isn't it grand?"

Then there was always your friend's house, where they probably had something important that your family refused to get, like a pool table, a dachshund, or a black-and-white car. There were also the book houses to inhabit instead of your own, which usually involved having no parents. In *Madeline,* Miss Clavel's boarding school for girls in Paris. Or Nancy Drew's house, with only a housekeeper and a red roadster, or Jane Eyre's cold bedroom as a governess. Or there was Ventnor Place, or your grandmother's house, and if all of these failed, there was the oak tree, and the highway, outside.

AND then there was Alabama. My brother and I knew the shape of every state in the union blindfolded, thanks to a wooden puzzle that my mother brought out on rainy days. Rhode Island, the tiniest state, was missing. But this was easily discounted west of the Mississippi River. Our state, Missouri, named like the beautiful river, was right there in the center, painted red. It wasn't the largest state, but substantial. Not a sinuous, tentative-looking shape, like Louisiana or Tennessee. A little fat and stolid. It was straight on most sides, but wild on the right side, the Mississippi River border. Underneath was Arkansas, dismissed by my parents as hillbilly territory, where city people like us would never go, even to fish in the Ozark Mountains. Underneath Arkansas was Alabama, which we believed was even more primitive than Arkansas. It was farther removed from the civilization of Missouri, which, my father pointed out proudly, had been a border state during the Civil War. All we really knew about Alabama was from the song about going there with a banjo on your knee. When my brother dug a hole in the field behind our house, one that was deeper and bigger than our kitchen at home, it turned out to be in the shape of a rectangle. One little rectangle stuck out of it like a leg. He named it Alabama because its shape, viewed aerially, would have looked just like the shape of Alabama in the wooden puzzle.

Alabama was a kind of clubhouse. My brother and his friend Warren dug it in two months with shovels and a rigged-up pulley system. He had the most reason of anyone in our house to need his own underground house, since my father could not stop telling him, in both spoken and unspoken ways, to do things the "right" way, whatever that meant. But by what standard? Always checking, always measuring. This level of critique did not apply to my sister or me, since we were "just girls," as it was said.

My brother had built a house of his own before, a weather station for meteorological instruments. It was mounted in a tower that stood above the back field. He wanted to be a weatherman. He wanted to be able to predict storms, sun, rain. First my brother and his friend Warren visited the weather bureau. My brother took a picture of the instrument shelter and proceeded from there to build one of his own, as well as the tower to mount it on. At home, he used a ripsaw to cut four or five dozen louvers for the slatted sides of the shelter. My father's role in this was elusive. He did not come to work side by side with him, but would occasionally look in, and helped him out when he came to a dead end. Then my father would almost magically come home from work with exactly the right thing. Some pieces of metal that the louvers just fit. Some angle iron to use for posts to tie the guy wires down. He left these out on a table where John could find them. When the shelter and tower were finished, they looked like they would have passed inspection at the U.S. Bureau of Standards.

Alabama, though, was a lot looser. It had to be. Its walls were ten feet of Missouri mud that crumbled at your touch. You could see a cross section of the terrain, featuring red and gray layers of mud, and sassafras and sumac roots right on the walls of his house. He gradually civilized it. Tamped down the mud floor and swept it off. Brought out a rattan easy chair with a slight hole in the seat. Then an old chenille rug. Then a box, with an enamel dishpan that he set up, with a small bar of soap, as a washstand. Like in the good old days on *Gunsmoke*. Then he crossed the top with beams and made a roof out of tarp. My father had supplied the beams and tarp in his mysterious way. The crowning touch was lighting for night-time, provided by a headlight attached to a car battery. He and Warren dragged these through the field.

You couldn't see Alabama from our house. That was one of its attractions. Once it was all assembled, we moved our collection of Pogo and Little Lulu comic books out there. You could stay out there in the middle of a brush field full of lightning bugs, after dark, and read them, in the rattan chair, your feet on the rug, in the light from the car battery. If your hands got muddy from pulling sassafras roots from the walls of Alabama in order to smell them, you could wash them off in the dishpan. We started to stockpile a little food out there, some boxes of Kix and dried milk, and Alabama became a combination root cellar, tornado shelter, bomb shelter, and child shelter.

When my three cousins from Iowa came to visit, it was the first place we took them. "Where are they?" the grown-ups would say. "Out in Alabama" would be the reply, and everyone seemed completely happy with this invention. I thought everyone's brother had built something like Alabama. But over the years, my description of Alabama elicited both wonder and speculation from my listeners. Never heard of such a thing. A treehouse where you brought lunch in a bag with the checkerboard, yes, but not a hole in the ground big enough to hold twenty, with a washstand and an easy chair. Every child wants a private place. Alabama seemed to be in another category, the invention of a child who had a very pressing need to get away, out of sight, to rest in the comfort of cool walls, with fragrant roots of Missouri brush.

IN the years that followed, my brother had more Alabamas, places both wonderful and terrible in their isolation. He went away to college, but left suddenly. He stayed at our house for a few months, often alone in his room for a number of hours that seemed very alarming to me, sleeping too late, or just sitting, trying to decide what to do, for hours, days. It seemed to relate directly to his not really knowing, when he was younger, about turning to the right or the left, or hammering the nail. He went to the local college, but spent a great deal of time sleeping. He did describe one of his assigned readings to me, *The Metamorphosis,* about someone who woke up one day and found he was a cockroach. It seemed like my brother was considering this as one of life's possibilities. He would stay in his room and stew, and I would come in to sit with him. I'm not sure what we talked about. I worried about him. I wanted him to do something.

Eventually he got out of that room and moved back to Missouri, to the same town where my sister had lived since she was married. He lived in a basement apartment for a few years and got a job with a federal program, helping old people find housing. He bought a motorcycle, met a waitress in a truckstop, fell in love, bought an old blue-and-yellow Sunshine bread van and made a house inside of that, a movable Alabama. He drove it to California with her. Lost the girl, moved back to Missouri. This time he found a country-house version of Alabama: a little house with asphalt siding, three rooms, a wood stove, a pump for water, surrounded by a field of Black Angus cows with glistening fur, and the clear hills of northern Missouri that worked up to the bluffs on the Missouri River. Here he stayed for many years, with dogs, cats, a corn and tomato patch, some in-and-out kinds of friends for company. My sister said he needed a TV on winter nights up there. He said he had a sleeping bag and a system for stacking wood.

He was known for never writing letters back, for having a disconnected phone, for an irregular and unlikely remembrance of family birthdays, holding and not holding jobs where he delivered or sold things. Once I visited him and was impressed with the beautiful pumpkin color he had painted his kitchen floor. There was a wall calendar from a feedlot and some goldenrod from the field behind in his kitchen. Now he had bought an old ceramic pitcher and washbowl, to use when he pumped the water from the well, an improvement on Alabama. I was taken with a little plate on the wall that covered up the stove vent, with a picture of a farmhouse on it. Surely this house was the same as the picture on the plate, and surely this house was the same thing as a home. It seemed to me that my brother had found the country house at the top of the brush field that I was always traveling toward, walking my pig to the state fair.

But more and more, as the letters got fewer and fewer, till almost nothing at all, I ceased to think of my brother as a live member of my family. He was instead a ghost in a field in Missouri. I began to think of his house as another Alabama, a state that had been inhabited by vacancy, remote and inaccessible to me, not a home at all.

WHEN I began to suspect that my father was in the last stage of illness, I tried to get my brother out east as best I could. He viewed visiting my father at any time as a trial. It was never clear how many purely happy moments the two of them ever had together. My brother says he remembers some, in transit. Maybe a Saturday afternoon when he and my father would drive to downtown St. Louis together in the car, to a plumbing supply or hardware store, so my father could pick up some washers or nails. The radio tuned to the Met Opera broadcast, my brother and father in the pink Dodge with fins. My father brought him along for the company. They didn't have to talk. They could just take in as much of the moving landscape as they wanted to, bricks and trees, grain mills and factories. My father, on his mission, in transit, was happy, not critical. But inside the house, under the pressure of observation, this kind of moment seldom occurred.

It took quite a bit to get my brother to come out. I cabled him money from a drugstore, since he was short at the moment. I waited while he made up his mind how to get from Missouri to the East Coast: plane? bus? train? Waited two days for him to come by train, with delays in Chicago, still making up his mind. I met him upstate in Albany, and we drove down together on a foggy night on a crooked road next to the Hudson River. During this drive my brother was restored to me from ghost to live brother. For the first time, we said that our father was dying, had always been dying, of a disease, the drinking man's disease. That he was not just William Powell in a movie charmingly filling another martini glass and really causing no one any harm.

On our last visit, we ate dinner together with my father at the head of the table. At breakfast, he looked at the newspaper and companionably ignored us, pretty much as he always had. My new daughter, now a bouncy one-year-old, chattered happily at him. We took pictures of the three generations together. My father had the same look in his eye, playing with my daughter, as we sometimes saw in old photos of him with his own children — a moment when he caught the delight of the new one, who was in love with dogs, trees, clouds, sun, everything. We lifted her on my brother's shoulders.

It was getting to the end of the visit. My brother asked my father if there was anything he especially wanted to do. My father said, well, there were a few really good tools from the hardware store that he wanted. My brother drove him to the hardware store, and helped him build a fence for some flowers in the back of the house. I was a new mother, preoccupied with having to pack up to drive north with a young child and leave my father behind to fade. My hands were full. For the first time, my brother and father made the sandwiches for me. My father looked upon this as an amusing feat of engineering, and wrapped the sandwiches carefully in wax paper. It was our last day together, and I can say that we did, on that day, help each other.

After my father died, my brother soon left the house that was like Alabama in the Black Angus field. He moved into town and rented a little house. Someone had given us a tip about an organization for adult children of alcoholics. My brother took it up. He went to meetings, sought out rooms, not empty ones, but ones full of other people, where he was welcome. Now he had a phone, a house in town, people who came to his house, asked how he was, a list of people to call next to his phone. In the next months to come, he could move back to his home city, St. Louis, and buy his own house.

He would buy lentils and make a soup that improved on an old family recipe, and there would be a friend to come and eat with him and talk with him. He would swim, and talk with others, and walk through his old city in a new way. He would go back to college to study rocks and plants, after twenty-three years, and swim right through his work. Like the possum who was not really dead in our backyard, he found that it was possible to get up and walk away. As the older brother, he passed this tip on to me, in the manner that he had shown me about breathing out under water, jumping fences, and stringing up two tin cans between adjoining windows.

Runaway

IN the years shortly preceding 1959, my sister read all the books by Albert Payson Terhune about heroic dogs, and persuaded my parents to buy a collie. She named him Treve after one of the dogs in the books, and combed his long black-and-tan fur until it was glossy. She also liked to cook things up. She had a kiln she could heat up on her desk, to make copper jewelry with a glaze baked on top. She preferred earrings and pins in the shape of leaves or birds, and she convinced my mother to make many trips to the art supply store downtown to pick out the new shapes. From little envelopes, she sifted out finely shaded glazes from powdered enamel. She made birds from red to russet, leaves from yellow to burnt orange. She also painted watercolors from the jumbo paint box. Landscapes with washes of sunsets, like Lake Michigan on our summer vacations, highlighted by pointy pine trees, were set to dry near her windows.

In those years she let her hair grow long, had cat-shaped glasses, braces, and a lumpy body covered in shapeless skirts, saddle shoes, and baggy white socks. She looked embarrassed when her picture was taken, the way most girls do at that age, so aware of their awkwardness that they'll do anything to avoid thinking about it, like develop an interest in tropical fish, or do millions of sit-ups, or pluck their eyebrows in the privacy of their own room. By 1959, my sister was sixteen, and changed into a swan. She was the one who sewed a yellow-checked gingham skirt for her vanity table. Now her focus was shifting from the fur of animals and the shape of leaves to the shape of women. She took double bars of Ivory soap and carved them into luxuriant nudes, with delicate, arched necks. Because her medium was soap, and she was so ambitious for the sublimity of her subjects, the necks often broke off. Something that could happen to a developing swan.

She read the directions for washing sweaters religiously from the Woolite box. She did not squeeze them, she rolled the wet sweaters between towels, patted them reverently, laid them out to dry, smoothing out the shape, fastening the buttons carefully, plumping up the cuffs. A girl was known by her sweaters, after all. Peach mohair. White angora. Navy-blue shetland. Someday in the future, black cashmere. She also saved the cardboard from behind my father's shirts, when they came back from the laundry, to use as drawing boards for her most sophisticated project, dress design. Here she used pen and ink, which seemed very suave and sophisticated to me. First, a pencil sketch. Then, a black ink drawing of a woman with a long, arching neck, a cinched-in waist, hair piled on top of her head, wearing something that could have been a variation of Cinderella's ball gown, or a wedding cake. A ballooning dress with tiers of flounces, or scores of flowers trailing down it. Ice-blue ruffles, or pink roses. The decision to be made: A V-shaped neck? A scoop neck? Empire or Princess waistline? Something with a little danger, a little plunge. Matching flowers for the hair. Apricot-colored shoes dyed to match. A cake, a confection, soon to be turned into the pinnacle: prom dress, wedding dress.

But wait, I thought. This was all getting speeded up too fast. My sister had always seemed a bit out of reach. She was eight years older, and always caught up in her own enthusiasms. Collie dogs. Spatter painting. Painting-by-numbers. Making cakes with four different colors of icing. Catching lightning bugs. Planting zinnias in the backyard. But now it was different. Slumber parties, where rolling your hair was the big topic. A vanity table, kidney-shaped, with a flouncy skirt, and a glass top, where her trophies were carefully arranged, a heart-shaped locket, a tear-shaped bottle of Jergens lotion, a mysterious thin flask of Shalimar perfume. She loved the name Shalimar. She told me I should always use a pumice stone on the rough skin of my elbows, and rub in a little lotion. For what? I thought. I was still wondering when I could get my own pig and wash it in buttermilk, as in *Charlotte's Web*. Or trying to figure out how I could possibly get my parents to buy me a pony. I mistook the scrubby field behind the house for an available grazing plot. I had heard that if an eyelash fell out, you should blow it away and make a wish. So for about a year I saved all my fallen eyelashes in a tiny wooden canister, intended for a doll's house which my aunt had given me. There were about ten of them by that time. I was saving up for the pony. Blow them all at once, get something really good, went my logic. Now I could see what was coming. My sister was saving up, with the fluffed-up sweaters, the sit-ups, the dress designs, but she was saving up for a man.

BY 1960, my sister had changed into the woman of her own design, with the graceful curving neck, the upswept hair, the arched eyebrows. Now she had other aspirations. She said she wanted to have six children. I could tell that she pictured herself standing over a steaming pot in the kitchen, with pointy little flats and a cinched-in shirtwaist dress. Her other main idea was to look like Scarlett O'Hara in a flounced ball gown, the one made from velvet curtains.

That summer, my Great-Aunt Charlotte arrived for her annual visit. This was always a festive event, because Aunt Charlotte exuded an exceptional amount of good nature and joviality. She was a Christian Scientist, and let you know that any of life's burdens could be borne. She had been a schoolteacher who married a widower and took on his sons as her own. She lived across the streetcar tracks on Hebert Street from my grandmother. When she became widowed herself, she moved in with her sister-in-law, Aunt Mabel, also widowed. They were both left amply endowed by their husbands, so decided to travel together late in life. After a trip from St. Louis to California, they never came back, and set up housekeeping together on Point View Terrace, in Los Angeles, with ocean breezes and an avocado tree in the backyard. They went on to tour the South Seas and Australia together, and took the kind of cruises where the passengers dressed up in costumes when they crossed the equator. They brought us wonderful presents from their trips, maybe a grass skirt from Hawaii, a music box from Switzerland, or a hedgehog toy from Germany.

Aunt Charlotte had a particular style of visit — she couldn't do enough for you. First we'd fetch her and Aunt Mabel from the airport. They had fox throws dripping off their shoulders, one fox head biting the tail of the next. They even had beady glass eyes. These fascinated and horrified me — how could my two sweet old aunts walk around with dead foxes for decorations? Then they brought out crystal mints from a purse that had a significant clasp on it, a hollow sound. We took them home. Aunt Charlotte liked to institute herself as a houseguest by taking over the household once she was there. She did all the cooking in order to give my mother a rest, and tempt us with her special dishes, more luscious than my mother's everyday fare. Aunt Charlotte brought out stewed chicken with dumplings, floating in gravy, and German chocolate cake, with both a nut and coconut filling, and chocolate frosting. She made elaborate desserts for us even though she was diabetic and couldn't eat them herself. She played cards endlessly, and listened to anything you had to say as if it were a stroke of genius.

When my sister was sixteen, she planted herself in the kitchen on the first evening of Aunt Charlotte's visit. There she was in pointy flats, a tightly cinched shirtwaist dress, and upswept hair, cooking up stewed chicken with dumplings, Aunt Charlotte's own dish. Aunt Charlotte didn't fail to note the significance, the point my sister was making here. She had outmothered my mother, more glamorous, more efficient, more rapaciously domestic. Aunt Charlotte paused in the kitchen, watched my sister deftly dropping the delicate dumplings into a steaming pot, and said, "My, so *capable*," admiringly. My envy knew no bounds. So capable. So much older, so beautiful, so *woman*. All I did was blow eyelashes around looking for horses, and my sister was capable of all those girl things. Smooth elbows. Tall cakes. Heart lockets. It only reminded me that I was still eight years old. If she was so capable, and beautiful, maybe soon she'd be set free from our house, the full house of the not-so-capable, and she'd be leaving me. There was nothing to do about it. Eating the capably made dinner was even worse, and afterward I retreated to the porch to play Monopoly with my brother, to buy a few more houses for Baltic Avenue.

IT didn't get better. Now she was approaching her last year of high school. A cork-backed bulletin board went up in her room that was supposed to hold important mementos, invitations, dried corsages. She gave me the goldfish from her school science project, since it was clear she had other things on her mind. There was hairspray on her dressing table. Many fights developed between her and my mother about eyeliner, hemlines, and dying her hair a lighter shade of blond. Her bulletin board started filling up. A dried-up orchid. Scraps of material from a favorite dress. Matchbook from Steak 'n' Shake. Little calling cards that had names of her favorite songs printed on them: "When," "Where Are You, Little Star?" or "Runaway," as if she were identified by her preference. A glossy black-and-white picture of Bobby Darin, who looked too slick.

Now she was in her senior year. When she looked into the camera, she challenged it to capture the portrait of irresistible womanhood she had so long plotted to be: the eyebrows swept up, the eyes deepened with liner, the skin a velvetlike matte, hair turned to the enviable ash-blond, black V-neck line, adjusted low, showing off a black ebony pendant given to her by every girl's dream, a steady boyfriend. The first time this boy picked her up for a date was a big event. She had let it be known around the house that he was The One. After dinner she locked herself up in her room, but we all knew what was going on. Searching the mirror for an errant eyebrow. Curling eyelashes, kicking on and off different pairs of flats, adjusting bobby pins. Then, the big moment, he rang the bell. I was too mad or too shy to be downstairs, but I stole a look from the top of the stairs. He was thin and dark-haired, with a deep sculpted face, but a little unformed and gangly, like Eddie Haskell. Black-and-white saddle shoes, green '51 Chevy coupe with red wheels. So, okay, what was the big deal? Boy-crazy, I thought. A boring waste of time. His name became her theme song.

I was snooping around in her drawers once and found more white cards, like the ones with names of songs. On these she had written out in pencil, like a future poem or a book projected, the names of her future children. She conceived them in long, ponderous syllables: Angelina Rose, Maria Angelina. When I found those, I knew my sister no longer lived with us. Now my sister made me a partner in crime for the first time. One night when my parents went out, she had a party on the sly for her friends, and that boy. She baked a pizza from a Chef Boyardee mix, which had just recently hit the market. I was supposed to be sleeping upstairs. She came into my room with her buffed nails, eyeliner a little more dangerous, smelling like Shalimar, with a plate in her hand. "I'll give you a slice of pizza if you don't tell Mom and Dad." Okay, I said. This partnership wasn't on the terms I had dreamed of. I'd thought we'd be comrades. Train horses together, jump in steeplechase races, jointly be Elizabeth Taylor in *National Velvet.* Only my sister was now the Elizabeth Taylor in *Cleopatra,* yearning toward the kind of eyeliner jobs that met at little points at the end. I still couldn't believe it.

When we were younger, she had pointed to another kind of sister act. She had an imposing oak desk in her room that had been in my grandfather's office on the corner of Grand Avenue and Hebert Street. It had bookshelves on its sides, which now held my sister's collection of Dell paperbacks. On one of them, in curvaceous lettering, it said *Jane Eyre* by Charlotte Brontë. "Look," she said, with her bubbling-over-the-pot enthusiasm, the kind that inspired cats to wave their tails, flowers to bloom, children to feel the world magic. "Look at this. Both of our names on the cover of this book. Jane. Charlotte." So I thought that's what it meant to be somewhere. Your sister and you together permanently on a book. Set in amber, set in print, forever, Jane Charlotte, Charlotte Jane, holding our hands that looked just like each other's. But her hand slipped right through mine, like the woman carved from soap with the delicate neck, Jane.

IN her last year of high school, my parents took my sister to look at colleges they thought of as the right kind of place: Washington University, the University of Michigan. But she wanted to go with her boyfriend to the state university. My parents were disappointed; this school was not one of the "fine institutions" of their dreams. The setup, going away with her boyfriend, looked bad. But they let her go anyway. She did college things, decorated her dorm room, fought with her roommate, tried out for sororities, went to football games. She aced her classes in French and Russian, wrote home letters full of exclamation marks, words written in the Russian alphabet, and asides about her boyfriend. Meanwhile, our whole household had moved east. When she came home for Christmas, it was to stay in my new bedroom with twin beds. This was my dream, that she would be my roommate. Having her there was like capturing one of those tiny blue butterflies, which I had tried to do the summer before.

A few weeks later, she called home with an announcement. She was getting married and dropping out of school. She was pregnant, she was thrilled, of course she wanted to have the baby. About a week later we were in St. Louis for her wedding, a hushed affair in the chapel of St. Ann's Church. A dinner followed in a room at a catering hall. My sister's face glowed, and everyone else's on both sides of the new family ranged from doubtful to stricken. They cut the cake, and Jane seemed to have enough bravado for everyone.

In the years that followed, she applied herself to domesticity wholeheartedly. Her husband was in college, they were broke, but she had, she said, "the most beautiful baby girl in the world." She scrubbed the floors of every falling-apart student apartment they lived in. She painted giraffes and balloons with her old oil-paint set on orange crates to make bookcases for the baby. She starched the curtains that she had sewn from bedsheets. She learned to make a beautiful sour-cream pound cake with a recipe from her husband's family. She embroidered daisies on the collars of her daughter's dresses and brought her to look at dogs, at trees, at books of Madeline running down streets in Paris and Mary Poppins floating away with her umbrella in London. When I visited, as a twelve-year-old aunt, she gave me some quarters to take my niece across the way to look at cows and eat ice cream. She sang, she ironed, she grew ferns in a pot. It all seemed perfect, but it all seemed a little like a high-wire act.

But she kept it up. Her husband finished college and went to graduate school. She wanted another child, dreamed of a boy, and had one, who suddenly, mysteriously, died three days after he was born. My mother was now dead, and I remember thinking that my sister was going to have no one to help her with this. She went back to the scrubbing and baking, holding her older child's hand on the way to the corner. Two years later, she had another boy, "the most beautiful boy in the world," as she said. Now she was completely happy. He was as bright as the first light of the morning. Her husband now had a good job, and he built a set of indoor slides for the two children in the sunroom of a handsome old house.

What happened next is what no one understood. It seemed that one day my sister was rolling out some cookies for her two children, and the next day she was gone. She took off on some path no one could follow. We could not bring her back, not doctors, psychiatrists, husbands, lawyers, ministers, children, fathers, brothers, friends, sisters. The terrible path of her illness included shock treatment, state hospitals, hippie crash pads, more husbands, children lost in divorce court, drop-in centers, back to college, lithium for manic depression, secretarial jobs, child-custody court, country houses. She got a job as a reforming social worker but was fired for rebellion. She lived in shacks by the river, state hospitals, trailer parks, slept in jails and on floors. She conned the shrinks, defied diagnosis, married again, took a job cooking at a truck stop, slept on ice inside her river house. She moved rhapsodic toward freedom, hurling glass and bones behind her.

She still held on to that boy's name, like a litany, as if it were a key. What did it ever mean? I wished that it had been my name, the harmless name of an old aunt who visited Hawaii and baked cakes, the fanciful name of the woman on the moors who dreamed up Rochester. But I was the more sensible Charlotte, the one who had looked bored and disgusted in pigtails, sitting on the edge of my bed watching my mother twine real roses into my sister's French twist. Trailing them through the curve of that twist, my mother did not look happy about her firstborn turning herself into a morsel, a confection, on the night of her senior prom, in a dress very like the ones she had drawn on cardboard years before. It was not my name that could call her back. None of us could call her back, and perhaps it was her own name, not even that boy's name, in the end, that called.

Through the sixteen years of her illness, she would cast off each of us and her children, wanting more from us than we knew how to give, wanting nothing it seemed except to be left alone, or to be called back, always at the edge. On the highway alone at night in a telephone booth with pneumonia needing cigarettes and calling collect a thousand miles away to send her some money. To send bail money, to send child-custody money, to send her a sweater, to send her some good clothes so she could get a job. When she did call it was the kind of call you couldn't answer. She had just called you to say her husband was after her with a pitchfork, had knocked her down the stairs, had sold all her stock money out from under her, had taken her children away, had forbidden her to leave the house, was smoking pot on the levee with her, was raising organic herbs with her, was playing the piano and throwing peanuts around the room, was making her rich in real estate, was spiritually aligned with her, was of one mind, was living with her and splitting to Florida with her, was drinking red wine with her. That Saint Cecilia was her bodyguard, and she knew more than the doctors.

We all had fantasies of rescuing her, but she was the recalcitrant one who didn't want to be rescued. She was my older sister, and had always known better. She'd been to college. She'd been a social worker. When she'd be in jail overnight, for some small thing, an assault in a bar, or writing a bad check, we'd think, at least she'll have to go to the state hospital for evaluation. They'll stop her, they'll help her, we'd hope. But she was very smart and knew the system. She was "of no immediate harm to herself or others," as they said. She was free. I would still think that if I'd sent her some nice clothes, she'd study French again. Hadn't she wanted to be an interpreter at the UN? We'd bake cakes together. She would part my children's hair with the same care that she had with her own children, that same care that had been taken with the part in her hair as a child. She would come back, the sister who sang to me, in a voice like a bell, "Sur le pont d'Avignon," as the last light fell outside on a field in Missouri. It was another wish.

The misery did not end, and there was only one insubstantial wish after another. Maybe a new climate. Maybe this new job at the truck stop. She says she wants to go back to school now. Maybe this new husband. My father was worn down to saying that the Salvation Army was a fine organization, that it probably wasn't such a bad place, that he had talked to one of the officers there only last week. My brother had been her sidekick, who looked to her for advice and inspiration in all matters. He thought her the most beautiful being in all of creation. But now he could only find her for Thanksgiving and Christmas, no more. I was the younger sister, who wanted nothing more than to have her call my name instead. Finally she did. For money, for court cases, for wine, for blowing apart the roof over her head, for running from husbands, for finding new ones. For sending me messages written half in French, half in Russian, long poems, rhapsodic advice on what to name my children, messages written on the back of fliers from an adoption agency, pictures of soybean fields in bloom.

The doctors called it manic depression. For a year or so, she had taken lithium. She had a house, held a job, and got custody of her daughter. It was like a miracle. But she started reading up on lithium in medical journals. There were side effects, no doubt. She said it made her fat and she couldn't think right. She stopped taking it. We thought she had the right to make her own decision. Now she called us out to her house, and her husband of the moment and she were having violent fights. He told us, "If you love her, commit her." We all agreed that he was a fascist, and that this sentence, this "if . . . then" proposition of his, did not make sense. But none of it would make any sense. Not her letters in Russian about soybean fields, not her leathery red face, not the reports from the medical "experts."

Now I was getting ready to have my first child and about to get married. If she came east for my wedding, I thought, my father would die on the spot. Because he would have to really look at his first girl now turned stray, he would have to ask, where are you living? He had a bad heart, and I did not think he could bear hearing the answer. Then I thought I would lose my baby from heartache, since I had already lost one in a miscarriage. I was also worried that if she traveled east, and she stayed with me, and I said something to her about drinking wine and throwing the kitchenware around at 5:00 A.M., she'd just say, well, you always were the family princess. And leave in a huff, broke and discouraged, get lost somewhere in New York, a viaduct, a subway grate, a park bench, a train station, where I could never find her again, where it would be worse than wandering in a small town in Missouri.

It wasn't what I would have wished for. I didn't wear one of those wedding dresses, like the ones she used to draw on the shirt cardboard, and I was not happy. I could not forget that now, my sister was the thirteenth fairy, uninvited. Jane Charlotte, Jane Beryl, Beryl Charlotte Jane, I wish I could have done better. I will try to become capable. I will try to find your children. I will care for my own, I will put our names together in a book. My daughter said she wanted one of those lucky cats, three colors, like they had on ships, like I had when I was young. She said she would name it Jane. It always seems there is more to say about this, and I know in advance, it isn't enough, song without words, world without end.

Eclipse

THE *Post-Dispatch* predicted a total eclipse of the moon at 2:38 A.M. It would have been at the end of the summer of 1960. I don't know who thought of it, my father or my mother, but someone decided that the eclipse would be a family event. They would wake us under our summer-weight patchwork quilts to come outside and view the night sky, the dwindling moon. I don't know their reason — maybe the national obsession with space. No one else in our neighborhood came out to do this. Maybe my parents thought it would be very educational to have their children see an unusual event firsthand. Maybe just for the plain beauty of it. My brother told me they had gotten everyone up for the northern lights a few years earlier. It seemed remarkable that they roused us for this, because our parents were relieved enough when we were asleep.

We made special treats in preparation for the event — homemade popsicles from Coca-Cola. It was hot, the kind of night you covered up only with a sheet around your middle. Two o'clock arrived, and my parents woke us up. Always proper when they might be seen by someone else, my parents were dressed and coiffed. The neighborhood — the curbs, streets, and sidewalks, which we usually shared with the Wilsons, the Krugers, and the Norbans — was all ours. We were excited. We ran in and out of the house. We brought folding aluminum lawn chairs out, trying not to scrape them too loudly on the concrete driveway. We checked on the popsicles. My father looked officious, heading this operation, standing at the top of the driveway, comparing the notice in the newspaper against his wristwatch. My mother was sporting, if sleepy. The streetlights made longer shadows in the late night. Our cat was surprised to have company on her regular night prowl, and ran in and out of the shadows, her tail pluming behind.

We had almost forgotten about the eclipse, the beautiful word, eclipse, and suddenly, we began to see the moon diminishing, like speeded-up film. From the old round moon to three-quarters. We ran back and forth a few times. Then a half, then an orange slice. We checked how the roots at the bottom of our maple tree looked in the dark. Then a thin crescent, then nothing in the moon's place. When the moon came back, it was time to go back to bed. My mother had not once wrinkled her forehead while she searched the sky for crows. My father had forgotten to look for a train. This was the moon, and the middle of the night, and what it could do for you. We were in some indeterminate space together, another zone of time. A total lunar eclipse that you could see on a hot night in St. Louis would not occur again for many years. We were all traveling together, the moon had filled our heads, we were not exactly there, any of us, we were not being obedient daughters or failing sons, or conscientious mothers or always-under-scrutiny fathers. We were there just as our original selves, the five moon-gazing animals, for 19.53 minutes in 1960. You couldn't tell me it was possible to be any happier than this.

Bittersweet

WITH much planning, Thanksgiving 1990 passes peacefully enough. But by the following day, it seems like some hot poison has filled my veins. I've landed in a hole, without noticing the descent in time to brace myself. It seems like I've been trying not to cry all night and my throat hurts from the effort. I get desperate thinking about where my sister used to be on Thanksgiving. At a Salvation Army church supper, or with friends, a turkey, and some cheap wine. A lot of cheap wine. I read an article about people living under a railway trestle in Manhattan, a guy roasting a turkey in an oven he'd made out of foil and an old filing cabinet. You try to read this like it was cinema, a colorful picture of a bunch of bums coming together under a tarp for a Thanksgiving meal, turkey in a filing cabinet. You try to read it that way, but you can't. It's your sister, the same one who sang you songs to get you to sleep at night, when no one else would remember to do that. The same sister who made Christmas cookies of thin iced trees with tiny silver balls, who sang "The Holly and the Ivy" with such fervor, her voice like bells. Who was so far gone at your father's funeral that her face was red and leathery from being out in the street, and from drinking bad wine. Who was so used to hoarding, so turned in on herself, whose position in this planet was so threatened, that she begrudged you, her little sister, a cigarette from her pack, in the ten minutes left before you were to take your father's ashes to the cemetery. Who died three years later on a tender, early-spring day, one of those cruel memory-and-desire days of Missouri April, from heart failure and chronic alcoholism, age forty-six.

In Thanksgivings past, no matter what else I was doing, later I'd get a wild, sick, animal feeling, not knowing where she was. Every time I thought about her, not just holidays, but worse on holidays, that feeling. Now, for the first time in many years, I can say I know where she is. I imagine for a minute that I could find her now, and just sit down at the table, and have a sociable, peaceful kind of holiday cup of coffee, a little catching up, a little gossip.

I can't get her off my mind. I imagine my brother is having the same problem. Thanksgiving was always hard. Sometimes he'd go to find her, and they'd eat a buffet dinner at the Holiday Inn. Two lost children eating hotel food together on a family day. I am sure he's wandering around somewhere wild with grief. I conclude he's left town, furious he didn't let me know, in case I needed him. I'm worried he went back to Columbia, to see old friends, maybe also to run into my sister's ghost, having turkey under a railroad trestle. Maybe he'll just wander off there and I'll never find him. Then everyone will be gone. No old father to carve a turkey. No old mother to retie her granddaughter's hair ribbon. No sister to pour a cup of coffee. I think about being lost and alone. I know it does me no good, it just leads to a big black hole, to walking around from room to room in a brick house by a field and a bad dream where there's no one else in there.

THE next day I get a little courage. I have a room full of old boxes and junk upstairs that I avoid because I fear coming across some old family memento. So the boxes remain untouched, for five years now. My children call it "the box room" as if every house has one, a room that their mother refuses to deal with. They even play in it, they say "Let's go play in the box room," and amuse themselves with old straw hats, a mismatched pack of cards, unwound clocks.

I am still furious about the holiday. I don't see how I could have done much more to avoid feeling swept away by grief. I swam my laps. I saw friends. I sobbed cathartically in my therapist's office the day before. But truly, there is no good answer, no good way to think about a beautiful sister, crazy at twenty-eight, wandering the streets at thirty-eight, dead at forty-six. It is still the first year of grief for her death, and the sixteenth year since her other death, when she walked over the side of the earth. Even now I can hardly write her name, because it is synonymous with tragedy, for whatever is surely and brutally without end. None of us could be her keeper, none of us could keep her from taking the path that her blood seemed to propel her on. We say this. We are told this by others. But deep down, none of us will probably ever believe that we couldn't have saved her. If wishes were horses.

MY sister's name was Jane. Her name is the same as anything you can't bear to think about. It means that despite waking early, or leveling off the flour in the measuring cup, or reading a story at dusk to your children, you cannot chart the course of someone's life, you cannot even be sure the perfect skin of your child won't become the weather-beaten, haunted cheek of a stray. It seems to mean that none of this holding on, my grandmother slapping down the iron on Uncle Ed's shirt, guarantees anything at all. I can't figure out how I am supposed to look like I'm enjoying this holiday, for the sake of my children, with this ghost walking my streets, having a cigarette outside my house on the curb, looking pissed off. Shouldn't I be mad, that I can't invite her to my table now? Even when she was alive, I thought if I did, the floor, the table, would swim and fade underneath me until I wouldn't recognize this side of the earth either. Because, after all, weren't my sister and I just alike? We used to examine ourselves to make sure. Same hands, we said. Same long fingers, not like my mother's, rounded, that had puffed over her wedding rings. Same long fingers, like our father's, good for fingering octaves on the piano. Same eyes, cat-yellow, that no one else had in our family, just us. Why shouldn't I be mad that I wasn't smart enough, transcendent enough, to know how to hold her, to call her back? But I was mad, too, that these were the impossible questions of being her sister, not simply what are you taking in your coffee, how are your children.

So this rage is creeping out, a little here, a little there, over the holidays. I cook soup and smell the fragrant steam from the carrots and onions, but I slam down the pot lid too hard. My child is on my lap, telling me about his new friend named Jane, and had I ever heard of that name, Jane? I take him off my lap and leave the room suddenly. I go to the box room, and sort through piles of old clothes, happy to throw them out. I feel very efficient, making order out of the dreaded box room. But then I come across an old box of papers and one framed photograph, and I think that my body will fall open right then, over this picture. I want to yell at everyone for making me look at this. It's my sister and brother, ages four and two, about the same ages as my own girl and boy are now. My sister, a beautiful clear-eyed child, with light in her eyes, maybe her eyes on a star. Her hair parted and brushed carefully to the side, clipped with a barrette. A white dress, with tiny cherries embroidered on the collar. My blond brother, a mild, good-natured face, open like any leaf to the sun or wind, not armed at all.

The picture always hung on the wall going upstairs. These were my predecessors, the beautiful, guileless children who lived in my house before I did. The picture used to irritate me a little when I was a child, because I had always envied their previous child-lives.

By the time I was born, they were already eight and six. They were a set, Jane and John, with matching letters in their names, which people said in one breath, JaneandJohn. Their child days always looked better, the sunlight sharper in the backyard. Once I came across a picture of my father dressed in a head rag and sash, like a gypsy, for a party given for them. It astounded me; my parents were now much older, and I had not known them to be this festive.

In this portrait, all hope shone forth from their eyes, and the hope of their parents, as well. They were the ones who parted their hair, brushed it till it was shiny, ironed the collar with the cherries on it, selected a quiet matching frame for the picture so the brilliance of their children's gaze could shine forth. They nailed it on the wall of their brick house so that everyone could see it every day or every night on the way up or down the stairs.

Now, here is this picture in my hands. What always seemed to belong to the rest of my family now belongs to me. For what use? Another reminder of the children so carefully raised, that I couldn't save, that resemble my own two children. It tells me that nothing is for certain. Two children, the twin despairing poles of my mother, hope and despair. The twin emotions of their little sister, envy and guilt. Guilty for that envy because the older girl so envied was eventually lost and died. Because the older brother became rebuffed into silence for many years. I wind up with the portrait in my hands, and not really one good memory to go with it, only many, many kinds of grief and sorrow.

My sister once told me, in her vagabond days, if it gets really bad, just get in your sleeping bag, like a moth in a cocoon, and stay there until it gets better.

I GET hold of my brother, finally. He's been at his new place in St. Louis all weekend. He's been trying not to feel too bad about the holiday. Did some repairs around his little house, took himself out to Thanksgiving dinner at a bakery that has a family-style restaurant. He says the holidays weren't too bad. Only his back hurts.

I tell him about seeing the picture. A bittersweet kind of thing, I say. "Bittersweet," he says. And this is the story he tells: "I was looking for some trees to plant in my yard. There was one on sale, standing by itself. With orange berries. I had forgotten the name. I realized I had seen it around, it was bittersweet. I thought about planting some. Then I remembered — Mom used to keep a vase with some dried bittersweet in it, on the piano. Do you remember that?" We are always trying to remember some neutral, pleasant detail from our childhood. "No? Anyway. Bittersweet. I remember thinking then" — he was eight — "that she kept bittersweet in the house because that was like her. It was her. It was the way she thought things were. Bitter, sweet."

He says he decided not to buy the bittersweet, even though it was a beautiful plant. I am stunned to think that even this early, my mother's view of life as the always foreshortened horizon was so clearly set in place that her eight-year-old son, the one with a face as open as a leaf, would read its limitations so clearly. Despite the house she furnished so carefully, the hair brushed so carefully, the picture taken so carefully, framed and hung on the way up to bed. I was sorry to think that my brother, with a face like my own small boy's, had to spend so much time keeping company with a woman he took to be the same as bittersweet.

I said I thought it was a very good idea not to buy that plant. I said, for the next holiday, why not buy something like those other families always had, a red poinsettia wrapped in silver foil, with a few Christmas balls stuck into it? Something really for the holidays, not bitter, sweet.

MY daughter's birthday comes a few days after Thanksgiving. Now it is time to come back from the not-holiday Thanksgiving. Time to make fourteen cupcakes with pink icing and ballerinas on top for fourteen little girls who'll soon come through my door. My daughter Anna's birthday. It would be nice if her grandmother, Beryl, the bittersweet, and her Aunt Jane, the vagabond, would stop in on this gathering. Maybe in the one moment when all the little girls stop chattering for a moment, and quiet descends, and the clock stops, that will be them, at peace, holding hands, smoothing a hair ribbon, admiring the party dresses, the cake that came from their own recipe box, and the fervent hope in the eyes of the birthday girl, named Anna Beryl, after Beryl Charlotte and Jane Beryl, as she makes her next wish. Maybe that will be them.

City of Bricks

ST. LOUIS, my city of bricks. Squat brick bungalows, brick French city houses with mansard roofs, brick warehouses, factories, steelworks, baby carriage company, sausage factory, brick houses with two stories and lazy porches, brick shoebox-style mean houses, brick storefront for the Pink Sisters of Charity, brick machine works, six square blocks of brick brewery for Anheuser-Busch, brick city market selling ham and live chickens, brick corner bar with a blinking Budweiser sign, brick thirties facades for vacuum cleaner repair shops, La-Z-Boy showrooms, neoclassical brick public libraries from the 1920s, granite cornices, thick columns, beds of brown iris lined with zigzag bricks in my grandmother's yard, oversized brick churches rising out of flat rows of tiny brick houses, brick row houses, brick water tower, brick firehouses, auditoriums, concert halls, palaces of culture, brick "Byzantine" movie theaters, ornate concrete moldings pressed down on top of them, a suburban brick house with a view to a field full of possums, milkweed, blackberry thorns, cottonwood trees, brick gate to the hills where my beloved mother, father, and sister lie with stones on their heads.

MY brother and I drive by this gate on the highway. I came to visit him for a day in the house he bought in Dogtown, St. Louis. A shoebox, shotgun house, just big enough for two people and a dog. He's going over his life and the city of St. Louis. He's moved back. He's walking in the streets, admiring the bricks. He knows all the details. He knows about an unusual kind of red mortar, used between the bricks in St. Louis, same color as the bricks. About some houses with green bricks, where the brickyards are, where the clay pits for the bricks are.

It's a tight little house. He keeps it tidy, the basement is dry, and it's his own. It's close to the zoo. Susan Sarandon just made a movie that took place in the neighborhood. Now that he's moved back, he spends some time going back to places, claiming them for himself. Our old house. My grandmother's house. The waterfront cafeterias, still decorated in fifties style with pink striped wallpaper and wrought-iron chairs, still serving coconut layer cakes and greasy chicken. I'm not sure about what he's doing, putting himself back in this landscape — flat land, brick houses, occasionally relieved by tall cottonwood trees with their fluttering leaves. My father lived at sixteen different addresses in his first twenty-four years, and he left a list of all of the streets he lived on in this city: Wise Avenue, Cora Avenue, Newstead Avenue, Penrose Street. My brother plans to visit all of them. He says the waterfront of the Mississippi River is a spiritual place for him. He says the Cahokia Mounds, right over on the other side of the river, in Illinois, give him a particular kind of rest, and he goes over every other week or so to sit on top of them.

I am not sure about all of this. I think it's one way of making the past clear, recovering the landscape for himself this time. He's stuck on these streets, I'm stuck in a story. For a while, at least. Both of us feel our missions to be necessary. He'll live in his own neighborhood now. I'll write my own story. He'll assemble his own idea of the city. He knows where the sources were, where the city was once water, where the train tracks were rerouted to, where there are warehouses for baby carriages, sausages, candles, and shoes.

He's planted a redbud at the cemetery. When it's dry for a long period, he goes out and waters it. I don't like to think about this, this solitary, once-lost boy driving out on a hot Sunday afternoon to water a redbud tree, his mother, father, and sister in the ground. He says it is sort of peaceful. That is just the kind of tenderness my parents would have wished on us. A simple, thoughtful, tending kind of peaceful. What they couldn't do. Their charges were not trees but children, bristling with joy and fear, desires and dreams, selfishness, foolishness, thorny loves, the normal difficult and bouncy material of childhood. Too much for them. They still needed tending themselves, the skinny boy turned head-of-house, the daughter pushed back to the window seat of a thick house. If only it had been as simple as tending a tree. My brother does this for them. He was always known in our family for having a generous disposition.

Maybe he's doing a better job of tending his grief than I am. I don't want to visit these graves. I don't want to fall on the ground, but I don't want to be distant and philosophical either. I don't want to be there at all. I don't want them to be dead in the first place, and presenting me with all this stupid grief. I want them to let me go, I want all these brick houses and warehouses and public buildings to let me go back to the place where I made a graft of myself. Where I finished school, found a job, got married, had children who seemed like stars caught from the sky, made friends, sat in peace on subway trains, ate first-rate jelly doughnuts and papayas, and wrote a book. Where I was listened to, where I found out that I had to learn to speak even more clearly.

I feel these brick edifices pressing upon me, finally, with the old, squashing messages: no, it didn't happen, be quiet, don't complain, don't bother your father when he's driving, he's tired from his long trip, don't ask him till he's finished his newspaper, till he's finished his drink, he'll feel better after dinner. Don't soar, don't fly. The brick house will keep you down. Mean, dark, the kind of little house that never gets blown down. Mean little pig that built that one.

MY brother says he can handle the graveyard. I say I don't want to go. He says, do you want to go eat lunch at the duck pond where we used to go when we were kids? I say, I thought about it. I thought about bringing my own children there to show them where I used to dream about buzzing dragonflies and castles on hills. I thought about it, but I thought I would not stop crying there. He says, maybe you should. I say, what would my children think, I would be taking them to see the happy place of my childhood dreams, and I wouldn't be able to stop crying. I had him there.

SO we bypass the pond and the graveyard. We go right to the airport, so I won't miss my plane. We have a long history of missing planes when we visit each other. The meaning of this is hardly obscure. As much as we are compatriots, just to be with each other reminds us of being stuck in that old time, that brick house. Not stopping at the pond and graveyard, which might make us late, cheers us up. We say it's possible to leap the past; our history is not just quicksand. Maybe we're getting a little better, we say. We go to the airport and it's crowded from my canceled flight. We sit across from the gate. We have extra time. Now we're getting into it. Heavy family talk. About how I make myself sick with it, even though I'm grown up, still being wound up, not paying my bills, having stupid fights with my husband, getting my daughter to school late, taking on too much to do, so I always feel like the demoralized child who just can't do enough. This is great, I think. I'll really break through. I'll never miss a plane, or deliver Anna late to school again. I'll just try to be normal, instead of transcendent. I'll stop annoying people.

While I'm having this revelation, my plane takes off. I probably should have gone to the pond, cried a salty sea of tears, like Alice, and maybe made it onto my airplane. I say to the bricks, to my brother, even to my mother and father, please, let me go. I am furious at my brother for not getting me on that plane, for not getting me out of there. Then I remember, waiting in line in a smoky, overstuffed air terminal: I am a mother of two, and a college professor. I should be able to remember to get on my own planes. I suddenly recall a recurring and very confusing dream of my childhood. I'm in the spacious backseat of a fifties-era car, the kind with a dome of a roof. It seems very far to the front seat. The car is moving downhill, and I look up and realize it's my brother in the driver's seat. But he's only nine or ten years old, with his child's face of hope and expectancy, a little confused, quizzical, wearing a yellow-and-black checked flannel shirt, or a flannel cowboy shirt, and it is very frightening to find it's only a boy in a flannel shirt behind the wheel of the car that is going downhill. The steering wheel is too big for him, his arms barely span it. It moves like an unwieldy toy, and now the car is really picking up speed, going downhill, or maybe over a bridge, wet and slippery with rain.

I could never figure out why my brother was elected in my dream to be in the position of authority, the driver of the car. How come it was never my father, or mother, or older sister? When I was the small child having the dream, they were certainly the ones that seemed more authoritative, my father the rise-out-of-the-cracks-in-the-sidewalk businessman, my mother the household saint, my sister the "capable" big sister.

Now this day at the airport I see something: I elected him to get me out of there because none of the other ones would be left. They're dead. I can't believe this. I can't believe I'm nearly forty, and I am also still that child in the backseat, stuck in a car sliding downhill, furious that no one is there to jump in and take over, throw on the brakes, tell my poor brother in the flannel shirt to move over, take his place, drive me to someplace safe. I can't believe the prophecy of this dream, and its relentless truth: my mother, father, and sister were not driving that car because they weren't up to it, and now they are not at the airport to see me off. They're under the redbud tree. They haven't been here for many, many years, anyway, my mother sighing, crow's-feet in her face as she scans the sky for clouds or bricks, my father thinking fondly about going out in a blaze of "white lightning" in Mexico for his life's finale, my sister walking the streets in long skirts and bells, who would have been better off, herself, being something else, a bell, or a river. So very restless, all of them, on this earth, but not put to rest either by leaving it. No happy ending, just another family tragedy.

My brother was behind the wheel because none of the others would live to take it up. But he was just a child, it wasn't really his job to get me out of that house, and it's not really his job now to get me on this plane. He says he's sorry, but he has to go to work and can't stay to wait with me for the next one. I can't believe he'll just leave me like this, but try to remember I am no longer in that dream and can get myself out of it. If I just concentrate on the next plane, if I do nothing but watch the clock for two hours, think of nothing else. The time seems to wind out longer than almost anything else: for a child to get itself born, for my mother to close her arms around me, for seeds to sprout in the damp and cold spring ground, for my father to get home from Milwaukee. To see if my husband who's late has been killed in the street or not, to see if the baby who's breathing twice as fast as he should passes the check for brain damage, whether the dog will lose his head and run in front of the truck.

I find a place to sit. I am begging this city to let me go home. Maybe I will miss the next plane, and the next, and forget my phone number, my face, my name, forget to put my hand to my head to check if I am there. Maybe I will forget my children, and wander this airport, become known as the woman who wanders the airport, trying to remember her children, her phone number, her head. Such things were known in my family, and really, what was the line between myself at the podium in the gabardine jacket, myself at the stove, handing my children plates of food, as a mother should, and the sister who's wondered, over and over, how she ever lost her children, whose hands looked just like mine, who sat up all night writing me rhapsodic messages in French, on napkins from Arby's. She got them in an envelope, somehow, those napkins with the messages. I wish I could have answered any of them, in any way at all.

But all I want to do now is get on a plane and go back to the place where I know what to do, where I feel safe, to the crook of my husband's arm, the nape of my children's necks, to another city where there is more trouble than anyone could ever imagine. I am begging these bricks, and these people, to let me get back there, certain if I ever do get on the plane, it will crash, since I have the good fortune to have a husband and two little children waiting for me. I remember not to get lost. I figure I might as well write about my trip. Is it a little crazy to write about your experience within twenty-four hours of having it? I don't care, because I know it's not as bad as a lot of other choices, and in fact it is what always set me free; my luck to have it. I remember my phone number, how to use the phone; I call my home. My husband and the children are still there, they are brushing the cat, they say, and making cold noodles with sesame sauce for dinner, and saving some for me. This must be paradise, and it is also my real life at the other end of the plane. If the plane doesn't crash, I can return. I can sing *bluebird, bluebird* to my children at night again. They will ask me, what does it mean, *bluebird, through my window,* and I will say I don't know, and they will say, sing it again. I explain to my husband, very embarrassed, that I missed my plane. He's not even surprised. He remembers what I forgot — I just made a trip back to my city of bricks, where I once was walled in.

The Possum's Story

I LOOK at old black-and-white photos of my parents. My mother sits in a field in California, the image grainy, like the weeds at her feet, her hair, her hands, her skin with the texture of weeds and her hair about to be tangled from the small wind ruffling through, the heads of poppies waving above her. In another one, my father leans over a bridge in Cambridge looking into the water, where currents are picked up by the sun. He's in profile, future-looking, inventive, thinking about building, what holds a bridge together. She would have liked to be a field, he would have liked to be a bridge, and I think I would like to be both, or at least the idea of them. I would have liked to have been sitting in that field, standing on the bridge, gazing in the same direction.

I find that these black-and-white outlines from an unknown era, my parents as light and shadow, fill me with an odd kind of longing. A mixture of loyalty and distrust, as if they inhabited a black-and-white film that offered a vague, murky kind of nostalgia to its viewers. I see images of a man and a woman, barely out of their twenties, trying to root themselves, trying to locate themselves in a world that seemed so very promising, a field of grass and flowers in California, a bridge in Cambridge. I would like to take them home. I want to tell them that those promises will be fulfilled, that the field-and-bridge-gazing restlessness will end. I now want to tell them that we will go forward with what we know. That I now know how difficult it is to put a field or bridge gazer into a brick house. That the faraway mother and the traveling man were completely different from the woman and man of these photos. I want to tell them there is an end to the longing "sur le pont d'Avignon," or " 'cross the wide Missouri." That the possum, who we all thought had died out back, who we thought we had to bury, was really alive. That he just got up and walked away. That I am trying to make myself into a bridge, into a field, over the silent and noisy rivers, to the place of connection, the man who looks for me in his bed, the trees that hold out their arms, the children who put out their hands, these places that are the luck of horses come to rest.